A SEASON TO REMEMBER

Ohio State's 2002 National Championship

The Columbus Dispatch

SP
SPORTS
PUBLISHING
L.L.C.

www.sportspublishingllc.com

Publisher
PETER L. BANNON

Senior Managing Editors
SUSAN M. MOYER AND
JOSEPH J. BANNON, JR.

Coordinating Editor
NOAH ADAMS AMSTADTER

Art Director
K. JEFFREY HIGGERSON

Interior Design
TRACY GAUDREAU

Cover Design
KENNETH J. O'BRIEN

Book Layout
JIM HENEHAN & TRACY GAUDREAU

Imaging
KERRI BAKER, KENNETH J. O'BRIEN,
JOSEPH BRUMLEVE AND
CHRISTINE MOHRBACHER

Copy Editor
CYNTHIA L. MCNEW

The Columbus Dispatch

Chairman, Publisher and CEO
JOHN F. WOLFE

President and Associate Publisher
MICHAEL F. CURTIN

Managing Editor/News
MARY LYNN PLAGEMAN

Sports Editor
DANNY GOODWIN

Editor
BENJAMIN J. MARRISON

Managing Editor/Graphics
KARL KUNTZ

Front Cover: Dispatch photo by Chris Russell
Back Cover: Dispatch photo by Neal C. Lauron

ISBN 1-58261-667-1

CHAMPION

INTRODUCTION

Standing before the cameras and microphones Jan. 9, 2002, a nervous Mike Doss announced to Buckeye Nation that he planned to return for his senior football season at Ohio State.

The Canton native said he wanted to do two things: earn a college degree, as his mother wished, and play for a shot at the Big Ten and national championships.

Coming from a guy whose team had just lost a bowl game to finish the season 7-5, the talk of titles seemed especially pie-in-the-sky. Every college football player in the country, after all, hopes to one day compete for the national championship; few actually get the chance.

The team's thrilling comeback bid against South Carolina in the Outback Bowl, however, convinced the players of their ability to compete. They trusted that, with proper discipline and focus, first-year coach Jim Tressel could shape them into an outstanding team—one that could contend for the conference title and the national championship.

And now, a year later, Mike Doss has lived his dreams.

The senior safety embodies the unselfishness that characterized the 2002 Buckeyes. Considered a strong candidate for the Thorpe Award (given to the best defensive back in the country) before the season, he assumed a different role that forced him to sacrifice personal statistics for team victories.

And succeed this team did, notching 13 wins (the most in school history) and no losses in the regular season.

"We were determined," Doss said. "We kept believing we could do it."

Despite some early blowouts, the Buckeyes had their confidence shaken several times. But whenever it appeared that they would fold and the fairy-tale season would end, they rallied.

Early on, the Buckeyes escaped a feisty Cincinnati team. Later, they trailed Purdue 6-3 with just under two minutes left before OSU quarterback Craig Krenzel, on a gutsy fourth-and-one play, threw a 37-yard touchdown pass to Michael Jenkins. They weathered overtime on the road at Illinois, Ohio State's first-ever OT game. And they came out on top against archrival Michigan—historically the Achilles' heel for any unbeaten OSU team—in a game that wasn't decided until the last play. With the victory came an invitation to college football's championship game: The Fiesta Bowl.

This was a season to remember.

The sports, news and photography departments of *The Columbus Dispatch* provided readers with day-by-day coverage of the Buckeyes' history-making 13-0 regular season, and their incredible double-overtime victory over Miami in the Fiesta Bowl for the national championship.

We're proud to bring you the team's remarkable story.

Ben Marrison

Benjamin J. Marrison
Editor, *The Columbus Dispatch*

Ohio State's Maurice Clarett slips past the tackle of Miami's D.J. Williams for a touchdown in the second quarter of the Fiesta Bowl to give the Buckeyes a 14-7 lead. (Dispatch photo by Fred Squillante)

MONDAY, AUGUST 2, 2002

OHIO STATE BUCKEYES

BUCKEYES HOPE THEY HAVE THE RIGHT ANSWERS

Seniors enter 2002 season focused on lofty goals

BY TIM MAY

These are desperate times for the 13 seniors on Ohio State's football team.

Players such as Mike Doss, Matt Wilhelm, Kenny Peterson, Donnie Nickey — they came in on the heels of two of the better teams in school history. The 1996 and '98 squads competed for the national championship and wound up No. 2 in the final polls.

Which is why, in the past three seasons—6-6, 8-4 and 7-5 campaigns—the Buckeyes have been judged harshly.

Although the team had some glorious moments last season (beating Michigan) and inglorious moments (blowing huge leads against Wisconsin and Penn State), coach Jim Tressel and his staff started setting the table

BELOW:

Ohio State's Scott McMullen (15), Craig Krenzel (16) and Andy Groom (18) drop back during spring practice at the Woody Hayes Athletic Complex. (Dispatch photo by Neal C. Lauron)

for a possible return to glory by attracting a highly touted freshman class.

But for the 13 seniors who reported Aug. 1 for the start of preseason camp, it's 2002 or never.

"The feeling that I have is if we don't go out this year and beat Michigan, or if we don't go out and win the Big Ten championship or compete for the national championship, I'll feel I'm missing out on something, missing out on greatness," said Wilhelm, who will be a third-year starter at middle linebacker. "It's something that was the reason I came to Ohio State, watching the '96, '97 and '98 teams.

BELOW:
Buckeye head coach Jim Tressel addresses the team at midfield after the spring game at Ohio Stadium on April 27, 2002. (Dispatch photo by Neal C. Lauron)

ABOVE:
Tailback Maurice Clarett runs with the ball during spring practice. (Dispatch photo by Neal C. Lauron)

ABOVE:
Buckeye running back Lydell Ross catches a pass during spring practice. (Dispatch photo by Neal C. Lauron)

"That's something we have a very good opportunity to do," Wilhelm said two days before two-a-day drills started. "We do have a way to come, but that's what these two-a-days are going to be for, to move along."

To make the run that Wilhelm and his classmates would like, starting with the Aug. 24 season opener against Texas Tech, they need to find answers to at least five key personnel questions:

— STARTING QUARTERBACK: Junior Craig Krenzel is No. 1 going into camp, and it appears it is his job to lose. Junior Scott McMullen, the backup all last season, believes he has a strong shot to win the job. And incoming freshman Justin Zwick, the most ballyhooed OSU quarterback recruit in 24 years, plans to make a bid that might pay off by mid-September.

— FULLBACK: The loss of Jamar Martin to the NFL meant there was going to be a major change, and the coaches seem to have settled on a Branden Joe-Brandon Schnittker tag-team approach after spring drills.

— OFFENSIVE LINE: Replacing longtime starters LeCharles Bentley, voted the nation's top center a year ago, and tackle Tyson Walter is the primary chore. The biggest question is whether returning starters Shane Olivea and Adrien Clarke, coming off injuries that kept them out of spring drills, will return to form a strong line with holdover guard Bryce Bishop and new starters Alex Stepanovich at center and Ivan Douglas at right tackle.

"I sat out all spring; there's a lot of questions roaming around about the offensive line and myself, also," Clarke said. "Right now, I'm just ready to quiet the critics and just ready to get started."

Stepanovich said, "That definitely has to motivate us, that everybody thinks we're the weakest part on the team. I think we should take that upon ourselves to prepare better and try to prove everybody wrong."

— CORNERBACK: As was the case a year ago, the starters will be new. Derek Ross left early for the NFL and Cie Grant has moved back to linebacker.

Otherwise, the defense is stacked, including the secondary, which boasts Doss and Nickey at the safeties.

"But there are answers," Nickey said of the cornerback questions.

Dustin Fox and Richard McNutt emerged from spring No. 1, with Chris Conwell, Harlen Jacobs and Bobby Britton providing depth and incoming freshmen E.J. Underwood, Nate Salley and Michael Roberts perhaps challenging for inclusion in the two-deep.

— FIELD-GOAL KICKING: Sophomore Mike Nugent hung on to the starter's job in the spring after a battle with sophomore Josh Huston. But Nugent was 50 percent on his field goal attempts last year (seven of 14), a percentage that Tressel would like to see improve dramatically. Expect the coaches to continue to develop a competitive atmosphere in camp.

As for the biggest overall question concerning the 2002 Buckeyes, Krenzel said it has little to do with a name or a position.

"It's consistency," he said. "Are we going to be consistent enough, play in and play out, offensively or defensively, and do the right things to make the plays, make some big plays, and not give up the big plays defensively?

"You look at us as a team this year and you can see we have all the talent in the world. The sky is the limit in terms of talent."

BELOW:
The Gray team's Mike Doss (2) tries to slip by the Scarlet defense on a kickoff return during Ohio State's spring game. Rob Harley (4) prepares to block for Doss. (Dispatch photo by Neal C. Lauron)

The Ohio State cheerleaders lead the football team onto the field before the season-opener against Texas Tech. (Dispatch photo by Neal C. Lauron)

SATURDAY, AUGUST 24, 2002

TEXAS TECH 21 AT OHIO STATE 45

STARTING OUT ON TOP

Freshman Clarett runs for 175 yards
as OSU makes statement with rout of Texas Tech

BY TIM MAY

Motivation came flying at Ohio State from all directions yesterday and the Buckeyes channeled it into a good-sized fist. The result was a season-opening 45-21 knockout of Texas Tech in front of an Ohio Stadium crowd of 100,037, the first nonsellout home game since the 1997 opener.

Such a one-sided thumping wasn't expected; the Red Raiders entered the Pigskin Classic as just six-point underdogs and the upset-special favorites of many experts.

But the defense stifled Tech quarterback and Heisman Trophy candidate Kliff Kingsbury. OSU

BELOW:
Buckeye quarterback Craig Krenzel (16) calls a play during the second quarter. (Dispatch photo by Jeff Hinckley)

That was the plan, Clarett said.

"I think it's just time for Ohio State to earn its respect back," Clarett said. "I think we lost it for the last couple of years, and I think it is time for us to put our foot down and say, 'This is Ohio State. We're back again.'"

Clarett delivered the mightiest blows for the offense. He rushed for 175 yards and three touchdowns on 21 carries (8.3 average), including TD runs of 59 and 45 yards. The latter came on the fourth play of the second half to up the OSU lead to 28-7.

The Buckeyes, who also gained two huge defensive plays to stop Tech scoring chances while outgaining the Raiders 477-372 in total yards, never looked back from there. But afterward they did, recalling moments that helped them construct a balanced and focused opening win.

Put out of mind were some of the distractions from the past year and preseason camp, which resulted in four players being held out of the game. Then came the surprising departure of a team favorite, fullback Jesse Kline, who opted to walk away from the game for medical reasons just days before what would have been his first start. Even Tressel admitted Thursday that he wasn't sure how the team would respond.

quarterback Craig Krenzel played with the aplomb of a big-boat captain. And tailback Maurice Clarett turned in the greatest opening-day rushing performance by a true freshman in school history. All that added up to the Buckeyes' 24th straight home-opening win.

"I thought if we got the chance to outhit them, we would," OSU coach Jim Tressel said. "And we did."

Freshman tailback Maurice Clarett outruns the Texas Tech defense for a 59-yard touchdown in the first quarter. Clarett gained 175 yards and scored three touchdowns in his collegiate debut. (Dispatch photo by Jeff Hinckley)

But he thought everyone was stirred by the pregame comments on focus and discipline delivered by former OSU captain Chuck Csuri, who gave up his senior year of football in 1944 to fight in World War II.

For Clarett, it was the team's pregame rally with the band in St. John Arena.

"It was my first time going to that," he said. "You just kind of felt the energy from the people screaming and hollering."

	1st	2nd	3rd	4th	Final
TEXAS TECH	7	0	0	14	21
OHIO STATE	14	7	17	7	45

SCORING SUMMARY

QTR	TEAM	PLAY		TIME
1st	**OSU**	TD	Ross 2-yd. run (Nugent kick)	10:53
1st	**OSU**	TD	Clarett 59-yd. run (Nugent kick)	5:10
1st	**TT**	TD	Francis 37-yd. pass from Kingsbury (Treece kick)	0:00
2nd	**OSU**	TD	Ross 1-yd. run (Nugent kick)	7:40
3rd	**OSU**	TD	Clarett 45-yd. run (Nugent kick)	13:08
3rd	**OSU**	FG	Nugent 45-yd. field goal	6:46
3rd	**OSU**	TD	Clarett 1-yd. run (Nugent kick)	1:56
4th	**TT**	TD	Welker 34-yd. pass from Kingsbury (2-pt. conv. succeeds) .	9:23
4th	**OSU**	TD	McMullen 1-yd. run (Nugent kick)	02:24
4th	**TT**	TD	Welker 36-yd. pass from Kingsbury (2-pt. conv. fails)	00:12

——— OFFENSE ———

TEXAS TECH

PASSING	ATT	COMP	YDS	INT	TD
Kingsbury	44	26	341	1	3

RECEIVING	CATCHES	YDS	TD
Welker	5	117	2
Francis	5	67	1
Paige	5	44	0
Peters	3	43	0
Glover	3	39	0
Munlin	2	10	0
Henderson	2	4	0
McGuire	1	17	0

RUSHING	RUSHES	YDS	TD
Henderson	3	31	0
Munlin	7	18	0
McGuire	1	9	0
Kingsbury	9	-27	0

OHIO STATE

PASSING	ATT	COMP	YDS	INT	TD
Krenzel	14	11	118	0	0
McMullen	3	2	42	0	0

RECEIVING	CATCHES	YDS	TD
Clarett	4	30	0
Jenkins	3	58	0
Hall	2	25	0
Gamble	2	11	0
Carter	1	26	0
Hartsock	1	10	0

RUSHING	RUSHES	YDS	TD
Clarett	21	175	3
Hall	13	74	0
Ross	16	40	2
Krenzel	4	34	0
TEAM	1	-1	0
McMullen	2	-5	1

But for tackle Shane Olivea, the focus became laser sharp on Texas Tech Friday night. The Buckeyes were shown a video featuring the highlights of brazen comments Tech players made about Ohio State in the weeks leading up to the game, more or less intimating the Buckeyes would be an average team in the Big 12.

"They got smacked today, and they can go back crying on their plane; that's pretty much how I feel," Olivea said. "The Big Ten, that's how we do it. I don't know how they do it in the Big 12. But it shows we can play football."

Tech coach Mike Leach found that out.

"The biggest thing I give them credit on, and that I feel like we fell short on, was just them playing together consistently," Leach said. "I don't think they had any real tricks up their sleeve, and we really didn't either. It was just base stuff and they executed better than we did."

It started with OSU freshman linebacker Bobby Carpenter tackling Tech return man Ivory McCann on the eight-yard line on the opening kickoff, and the defense forcing a punt from the five. It continued with Mike Doss returning that punt 14 yards to the Tech 32, Krenzel hitting first a 17-yard pass to Michael Jenkins and then scrambling nine yards for a first down at the four.

Two plays later, Lydell Ross scored the first of his two touchdowns and the Buckeyes never trailed. Clarett followed with his 59-yard TD run. And after Kingsbury found Carlos Francis for a 37-yard TD pass on a fourth-and-two play, the Buckeyes answered with a Clarett-powered drive capped by a one-yard Ross TD run.

Tech seemed intent on making it a game by driving to the OSU one late in the half. But on fourth and goal, OSU linebacker Matt Wilhlem shot the gap and corralled Foy Munlin for no gain.

Clarett's 45-yard TD run got the second half off to a good start, followed by the defensive play that broke the Red Raiders' collective back. Cornerback Dustin Fox made a diving interception at the goal line of a lob from a scrambling Kingsbury, and the Buckeyes drove to a 45-yard field goal by Mike Nugent. Win No. 1 was in the bag.

"This is definitely a statement game for the 2002 Buckeyes," Wilhelm said of the nationally televised game. "From the get-go to the end of the game, to the singing with the band, this is what you're going to see week in and week out."

RIGHT:

Maurice Clarett breaks away from Texas Tech's Ricky Sailor for a touchdown in the second half. (Dispatch photo by Jeff Hinckley)

LEFT:

Ohio State's Dustin Fox steals a pass intended for Texas Tech's Nehemiah Glover in the Red Raiders' end zone. (Dispatch photo by Mike Munden)

ABOVE:

Maurice Clarett is congratulated by teammates Santonio Holmes (17), Jesse Kline (29), Mike Doss (2), and Kenny Peterson (97) after scoring the Buckeyes' second touchdown on a 59-yard run. (Dispatch photo by Karl Kuntz)

BELOW:

Quarterback Craig Krenzel escapes a tackle by Texas Tech's Adell Duckett during the third quarter. (Dispatch photo by Mike Munden)

RIGHT:

Maurice Clarett celebrates with a teammate after scoring his first collegiate touchdown. (Dispatch photo by Jeff Hinckley)

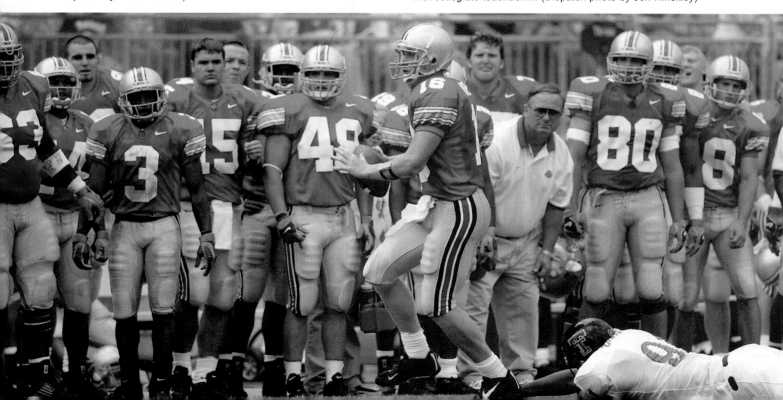

66 *IT WAS MY FIRST TIME GOING TO [A PREGAME PEP RALLY]. YOU JUST KIND OF FELT THE ENERGY FROM THE PEOPLE SCREAMING AND HOLLERING.* 99

—OHIO STATE TAILBACK MAURICE CLARETT

Franklin County Deputy Mark Ely salutes the flag before kickoff at Ohio Stadium. The Buckeyes opened the season Aug. 24 against Texas Tech. (Dispatch photo by Neal C. Lauron)

SATURDAY, SEPTEMBER 7, 2002

KENT STATE 17 AT OHIO STATE 51

38 AND OUT FOR KENT

Ohio State's early onslaught sets table for win No. 2

BY TIM MAY

If Kent State was going to have any chance at all in its first game against Ohio State, it was going to have to survive the start.

It did not.

On the strength of a punt block by safety Donnie Nickey, the first interception return for a touchdown by All-American safety Mike Doss, and pinpoint accuracy by quarterback Craig Krenzel, the Buckeyes ambushed their in-state little brother at the beginning and went on to a 51-17 win yesterday. It was OSU's first 50-plus scoring day since a 72-0 win over Pittsburgh in the second game of 1996.

BELOW:
Brutus Buckeye and the Ohio State cheerleaders lead the charge at Ohio Stadium as the team takes the field against Kent State.

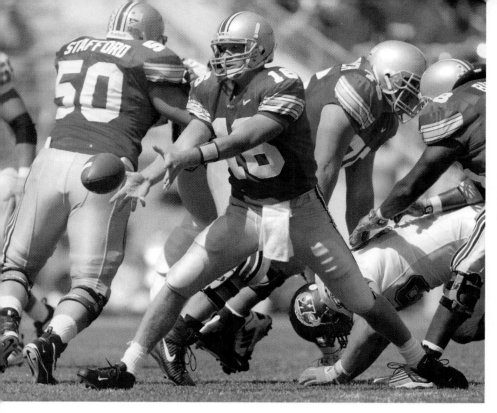

Few people expected Kent State to give the Buckeyes much of a game, as evidenced by the smallest crowd—98,689—in Ohio Stadium since it was expanded to hold just over 100,000 three years ago.

But the Golden Flashes, 28-point underdogs, could have hoped to catch the Buckeyes looking forward to their next game, a highly anticipated home matchup with Washington State.

It didn't happen.

"I thought in general, with the big one coming up next weekend, that our guys did a good job getting ready and taking on the task at hand, and jumping on

ABOVE:
Buckeyes defenders Matt Wilhelm (35) and Darrion Scott (56) work together to make yardage hard to come by for Kent State's Eddie Beccles. (Dispatch photo by Fred Squillante)

top and finishing the job," OSU coach Jim Tressel said.

Nickey provided the first punch when he partially blocked Jared Fritz's punt to give OSU the ball at the Kent State 31-yard line. Five plays later, Maurice Clarett plunged two yards for a touchdown.

Then, five plays into what appeared to be a promising Kent State possession, quarterback Joshua

RIGHT:
Buckeye defenders Tim Anderson (left) and Robert Reynolds (44) pressure Kent State quarterback Joshua Cribbs. (Dispatch photo by Fred Squillante)

	1st	2nd	3rd	4th	Final
KENT STATE	0	14	0	3	17
OHIO STATE	21	17	3	10	51

SCORING SUMMARY

QTR	TEAM	PLAY		TIME
1st	**OSU**	TD	Clarett 2-yd. run (Nugent kick)	12:16
1st	**OSU**	TD	Doss 45-yd. interception return (Nugent kick)	9:21
1st	**OSU**	TD	Hall 28-yd. run (Nugent kick)	4:35
2nd	**OSU**	TD	Clarett 7-yd. pass from Krenzel (Nugent kick)	13:57
2nd	**OSU**	FG	Nugent 40-yd. field goal	9:05
2nd	**OSU**	TD	Hawk 34-yd. interception return (Nugent kick)	7:31
2nd	**KSU**	TD	Moore 28-yd. pass from Cribbs (Mayle kick)	3:11
2nd	**KSU**	TD	King 8-yd. pass from Cribbs (Mayle kick)	0:24
3rd	**OSU**	FG	Nugent 33-yd. field goal	11:49
4th	**OSU**	FG	Nugent 45-yd. field goal	14:56
4th	**KSU**	FG	Mayle 33-yd. field goal	8:25
4th	**OSU**	TD	Hamby 18-yd. pass from McMullen (Nugent kick)	4:09

OFFENSE

KENT STATE

PASSING	ATT	COMP	YDS	INT	TD
Cribbs	31	14	160	2	2
Polk	4	3	27	0	0

RECEIVING	CATCHES	YDS	TD
Dowery	7	68	0
Moore	3	48	1
Kemp	2	17	0
Medley	1	20	0
Coley	1	15	0
Buckosh	1	9	0
King	1	8	1
Beccles	1	2	0

RUSHING	RUSHES	YDS	TD
Cribbs	21	94	0
King	9	34	0
Newton	6	23	0
Beccles	9	20	0

OHIO STATE

PASSING	ATT	COMP	YDS	INT	TD
Krenzel	14	12	190	0	1
McMullen	11	7	78	0	1

RECEIVING	CATCHES	YDS	TD
Gamble	6	87	0
Jenkins	4	89	0
Hamby	2	29	1
Carter	2	17	0
Clarett	2	16	1
Childress	1	14	0
Hartsock	1	8	0
Ross	1	8	0

RUSHING	RUSHES	YDS	TD
Clarett	11	66	1
Hall	3	36	1
Ross	4	28	0
Krenzel	2	11	0
Riley	2	3	0

Cribbs fired high on a rollout pass. Doss grabbed it near the east sideline and ran a diagonal route toward the west goal line pylon on his 45-yard touchdown return.

"It set up like a sweep; all 10 guys were blocking somebody," Doss said.

After the defense forced a three and out on KSU's next possession, Krenzel—on the way to completing 11 straight passes to start the game—found Chris Gamble on a 33-yarder that pushed the Buckeyes back into Flashes territory. Two plays later, Maurice Hall cut up behind Shane Olivea's block and sprinted 28 yards for a TD that put the Buckeyes on top 21-0.

Asked what he'd call such an opening blitz, Nickey shrugged.

"I don't know," he said. "Good football."

Golden Flashes coach Dean Pees had given his team the storm warning in the locker room. Ohio State's players had made no secret of their desire to deliver an early knockout blow.

"I tried to tell these guys that it wasn't going to be won or lost in the first five minutes," Pees said. "But the problem of it is that you have to be able to overcome some things and not drop your head."

By the 7:31 mark of the second quarter, after Krenzel hit Clarett on a seven-yard swing pass for a TD, Mike Nugent hit the first of his three field goals, and freshman linebacker A. J. Hawk celebrated his first collegiate interception return for a touchdown, the Flashes were down 38-0.

That Cribbs rallied them to two touchdowns—the second after a Hall fumble—before halftime was laudable, OSU defensive end Darrion Scott said.

"Going out there and probably thinking you're not going to win at that point but still going out there and playing 60 minutes of football without giving up makes me respect them a lot," Scott said.

After the disastrous start, Kent State switched to a spread offensive look. The Buckeyes had trouble adjusting to it, allowing the Flashes to control the ball

BELOW:
Ohio State kicker Mike Nugent boots the extra point after A. J. Hawk's second-quarter touchdown. (Dispatch photo by Mike Munden)

RIGHT:
Maurice Hall earns a chest bump from teammate Maurice Clarett after Hall's first-quarter touchdown. (Dispatch photo by Mike Munden)

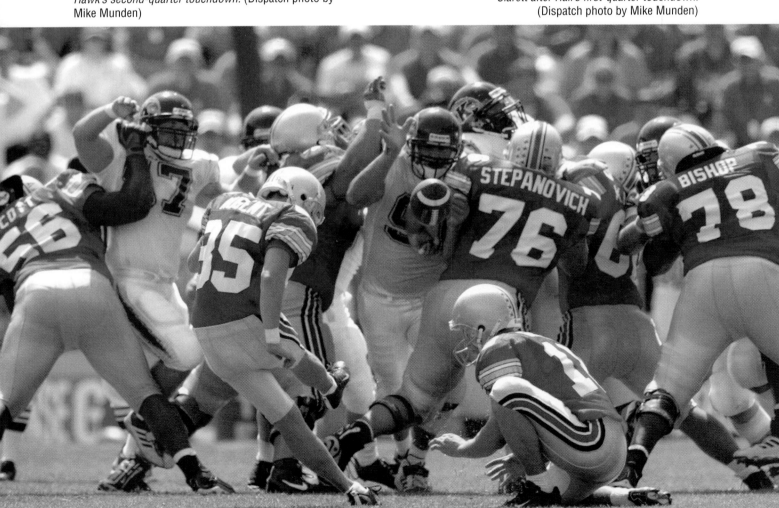

ABOVE:
Buckeyes safety Mike Doss brings down Golden Flashes quarterback Joshua Cribbs in the fourth quarter.
(Dispatch photo by Fred Squillante)

for an astounding 39:12 of the game. And OSU only outgained them 412-358 in total yards.

"If they hadn't scored anything, we could say we came out early and slammed them right away," Nickey said. "But they got points on us right before halftime and kind of stole the momentum from us a little bit."

However, Kent State never came close to making it a real game in the second half. The Buckeyes played keep-away with two Nugent field goals, including a 45-yarder that tied his career best.

The crowning blow came with the Buckeyes facing fourth and two at the KSU 18 with 4:14 left. Backup quarterback Scott McMullen hit tight end Ryan Hamby on a TD pass that pushed OSU over the 50 mark.

Pees was not upset.

"It's fourth and two. Go for it," he said. "Jim would have been criticized if he went for a field goal. Line up and play. If you don't like that, don't show up."

RIGHT:
Buckeye tight end Ryan Hamby scores on an 18-yard pass from backup quarterback Scott McMullen in the fourth quarter. (Dispatch photo by Fred Squillante)

LEFT:
Maurice Clarett dives into the end zone for a TD early in the second quarter. (Dispatch photo by Fred Squillante)

BY BOB HUNTER, COLUMBUS DISPATCH COLUMNIST

MAURICE CLARETT

13

Jim Tressel was pacing in the Michigan-tramping footsteps of Francis Schmidt, Woody Hayes and Earle Bruce on the Ohio Stadium sidelines Nov. 23. Maurice Clarett was following him, almost stalking him, and, well, talking.

Even when Clarett isn't playing in the biggest Ohio State-Michigan game in years, he's still the best damned sports show, period.

The Game has never seen anything quite like The Kid.

"I'm like Keyshawn [Johnson]," Clarett said. "I want the ball. I want the ball bad. I just have to drive to get the ball. When you work hard all week, when you work hard all season, game time you have the chance to perform and you want the ball so bad. I just want the ball."

Opponents try to catch him, Tressel tries to shake him, but neither has much success. Clarett is not only the best football player Ohio State has seen in years, he's also the best story. He wants the ball, he wants to play, he wants to win and he doesn't disappoint.

Ohio State 14, Michigan 9? Let's not kid ourselves. This doesn't happen without him.

"I think he [Tressel] hears me," Clarett said. "I don't know if he listens to me, but he hears me. He doesn't give me his attention, but . . . hey, I might hear the band, but I don't listen to them."

Tressel hears. The biggest offensive play of the Michigan game, a 26-yard pass from Craig Krenzel to Clarett to the Wolverine six-yard line with 4:55 remaining that set up the winning touchdown, was one Clarett had been lobbying his coach for since early in the game.

The squeaky wheel gets the grease, especially when it's powered by rocket fuel.

"He told me two quarters earlier," Tressel said. "He said, 'You'd better call that play. They can't check me.' So we waited until the opportune time."

Clarett didn't know what the play was called. He couldn't explain where he stood on Krenzel's progression list. He didn't know, he didn't care, and you could understand.

"I've been catching footballs since I was five, six, seven years old, so to me, it's like playing street football," Clarett said. "It's the same thing over and over again. Football is the same no matter which arena you play in, what kind of surface you play on; football is football.

CLASS: FR.

AGE: 19

HOMETOWN: YOUNGSTOWN, OH

TAILBACK

"You throw, you have to get first downs, you have to score, the people with the most points win. So when he threw the ball to me, it was kind of like a street football play, he just threw it up there, go catch it."

The ensuing option play that resulted in a three-yard Maurice Hall touchdown run? Get this: Clarett had been lobbying for that, too.

"On a couple of fourth and shorts I kept on telling him to run the option play," he said.

If you didn't already know that there is something different about this freshman, the Michigan game certainly should have clued you in. Clarett sat out the previous week's game against Illinois to give the painful stinger to his shoulder more time to heal, and he didn't start against Michigan. He took a hit on that shoulder on a 17-yard run in the second quarter that doubled him over in pain, even though trainers had him packaged like a piece of fine crystal.

"There are like four gadgets under my shirt," Clarett said. "And then I've got the hard covering over my bicep, and there is another pad over my AC joint. It's kind of crazy."

This story is crazy. He's a freshman, he's in constant pain and he gains 119 yards on 20 carries in The Game, including a touchdown and a game-longest 28-yard run from scrimmage. He also caught two passes for 35 yards, including the Buckeyes' biggest gainer of the game.

Thank God he got a good night's rest.

"I couldn't go to sleep," Clarett said. "We went to Chris Conwell's and Nate Salley's room, and these cats until like one in the morning are playing music and having a good time. It was funny. It was like they weren't even taking the game serious. But I was like, 'OK, this is the way they relax.' I was relaxing across there until about three in the morning, and finally went across to the room and tried to go to sleep, but I fell asleep at like 4:30.

"They were playing music, having a good time, talking on the phone. It was crazy. I think our wakeup call was like 7:15."

So he was tired?

"Nah," he said. "The energy just kept going."

No kidding. He didn't stop stalking Tressel until the end.

"When there are four minutes to go, Maurice said to me, 'How come the clock goes so slow when you're ahead?'" Tressel said.

"And I said, 'That's just the way it is.'"

See how this is? Tressel not only hears the band, but he also listens to it. The music has never been sweeter.

SATURDAY, SEPTEMBER 14, 2002

WASHINGTON STATE 7 AT OHIO STATE 25

OSU, CLARETT WIN IN A RUSH

Freshman runs for 230 yards as Buckeyes whip Cougars

BY TIM MAY

The way freshman tailback Maurice Clarett rose in the second half yesterday to lead sixth-ranked Ohio State to a 25-7 win over No. 10 Washington State was . . . well, it was . . .

"Unbelievable?" Ohio State offensive coordinator Jim Bollman offered. "Give him the ball and run out of the way. Just give him a place—I mean, he put it in his mind he was going to gain some yards, didn't he? And he did that."

In ripping off a 44-yard yard run that started the third quarter and shook the Buckeyes out of the doldrums of a 7-6 halftime deficit, and in rushing for

BELOW:

Ohio State's Maurice Clarett runs past the Washington State defense for 44 yards in the third quarter. Clarett totaled 230 yards on 31 carries. (Dispatch photo by Eric Albrecht)

ABOVE:
Buckeyes defensive end Darrion Scott sacks Washington State's Jason Gesser in the fourth quarter.
(Dispatch photo by Robert Caplin)

two touchdowns and 230 yards overall, the freshman phenom made it clear he wasn't doing it for the television exposure or the headlines.

For the people way up in D-deck to the folks down low in the end-zone seats, "I try to work hard for every fan," Clarett said.

In that case, he picked quite the stage yesterday, in front of the largest crowd—104,553—in Ohio Stadium history. But he didn't want to take a bow by himself. He said the win over WSU (2-1), considered the favorite in some circles to win the Pacific-10 this year, was a bold statement for all of the Buckeyes (3-0).

"Everybody's talked about getting respect back for the program," Clarett said. "I think in the second half we showed we were the better team."

Outgained by 80 yards—and probably a bad snap on a field-goal try away from being outscored 10-6—in the first half, the OSU defense throttled WSU's talented quarterback, Jason Gesser, and his spread offense in the second half.

"We wanted our defense just to keep coming at 'em, coming at 'em, coming at 'em," OSU coach Jim Tressel said.

Then on offense, well, as Bollman said, the rally plan was pretty simple. Give the ball to Clarett, do some blocking and get out of the way. With the Buckeyes gaining their first possession of the half on their own nine after a WSU punt, the plan paid dividends immediately.

Clarett took a deep handoff to the left and sidled up behind pulling right guard Bryce Bishop before reading his block and bouncing to the outside. He accelerated up the WSU sideline for 44 yards before being caught.

Three plays later, quarterback Craig Krenzel threw his only completion of the second half. It was a 14-yard gain to Chris Vance, who was making his first appearance after having to sit out the first two games for disciplinary reasons. Three plays after that, Krenzel scrambled five yards to the WSU 23 to keep the drive alive on a third and three.

Clarett, with some help from his linemen, did the rest. He ran through WSU defender Jason David on a 20-yard run, then snuggled in behind right tackle Shane Olivea and fullback Brandon Schnittker to gain the final three and the touchdown. It gave Ohio State the lead for good at 13-7.

The momentum turned decisively, Krenzel said, because of "the fact that we came out and we took it all the way down the field, and we ran the ball well, and we kind of did what we wanted to do coming into the game.

BELOW:
Ohio State's Lydell Ross rushes for 36 yards on a draw play before being tackled by Washington State's Jason David in the second quarter. (Dispatch photo by Chris Russell)

	1st	2nd	3rd	4th	Final
WASHINGTON STATE	7	0	0	0	7
OHIO STATE	3	3	12	7	25

SCORING SUMMARY

QTR	TEAM	PLAY		TIME
1st	**OSU**	FG	Nugent 43-yd. field goal	13:19
1st	**WSU**	TD	Darling 5-yd. pass from Gesser (Dunning kick)	8:33
2nd	**OSU**	FG	Nugent 43-yd. field goal	12:09
3rd	**OSU**	TD	Clarett 3-yd. run (Nugent kick)	8:37
3rd	**OSU**	FG	Nugent 45-yd. field goal	1:57
3rd	**OSU**	SFT	TEAM safety	0:47
4th	**OSU**	TD	Clarett 1-yd. run (Nugent kick)	10:41

——— OFFENSE ———

WASHINGTON STATE

PASSING	ATT	COMP	YDS	INT	TD
Gesser	44	25	247	2	1
Henderson	1	1	16	0	0

RECEIVING	CATCHES	YDS	TD
Lunde	8	64	0
Darling	6	65	1
Bush	6	63	0
Smith	2	38	0
Henderson	2	23	0
Green	1	5	0
Tippins	1	5	0

RUSHING	RUSHES	YDS	TD
Tippins	8	35	0
Smith	6	12	0
Green	3	0	0
Gesser	3	-5	0
TEAM	2	-25	0

OHIO STATE

PASSING	ATT	COMP	YDS	INT	TD
Krenzel	10	4	71	0	0

RECEIVING	CATCHES	YDS	TD
Jenkins	2	49	0
Vance	1	14	0
Gamble	1	8	0

RUSHING	RUSHES	YDS	TD
Clarett	31	230	2
Ross	10	46	0
Krenzel	8	19	0
Hall	3	1	0
TEAM	2	-4	0

ABOVE:
Cougars quarterback Jason Gesser tries to slip past Buckeyes defender Donnie Nickey (25) in the second quarter.
(Dispatch photo by Eric Albrecht)

"I think that's when the guys started feeling, 'Hey, we can just take it at 'em. We're going to wear them down. Our defense is going to play a solid second half, and we're going to win.'"

That appeared to be the case, WSU defensive end Isaac Brown said.

"I tip my hat to Ohio State," Brown said. "They came out and blocked way better than they had in the first half."

Clarett had 73 yards on four carries on the 91-yard drive and was well on his way to 194 for the half.

To put that in perspective, he rushed for 175 yards in the season opener against Texas Tech in what was considered a rousing collegiate debut.

Yesterday, though, he jumped into the 200 realm. Only one other OSU freshman has rushed for more in one game, eventual two-time Heisman Trophy winner Archie Griffin, who went for 239 against North Carolina 30 years ago. And Clarett's was the sixth best rushing game ever by an OSU back.

Also starring for Ohio State was kicker Mike Nugent, who kicked three field goals of more than 40 yards.

LEFT:
Ohio State defenders Cie Grant (6), Donnie Nickey (25) and E.J. Underwood (49) chase the football after a second-quarter fumble by Washington State quarterback Jason Gesser. (Dispatch photo by Barth Falkenberg)

BELOW:
Buckeyes quarterback Craig Krenzel runs for eight yards in the third quarter, passing Cougar defenders Virgil Williams (24) and Marcus Trufant (45). (Dispatch photo by Chris Russell)

In all, the Buckeyes outgained the Cougars 363-280 in total yards, with 292 of OSU's yards coming on the ground. And the OSU defense befuddled Gesser with defensive plays that ranged from two defensive tackles—David Thompson and Tim Anderson—breaking up passes downfield out of zone-blitz plays to linebacker Matt Wilhelm and freshman safety Tyler Everett snagging spectacular interceptions.

The defense answered the bell against an acclaimed passing quarterback for the second time in three games,

complementing the way the Buckeyes controlled Texas Tech's Kliff Kingsbury in the opener.

"That's something Coach [Mark] Dantonio talks about, that every week we're going to have to go out and stop a great player," Wilhelm said.

The difference yesterday was that Washington State could not stop Clarett when it mattered.

"We were trying to go to about 12 guys on defense there in the second half, putting 13 of them up there as defensive linemen," WSU coach Mike Price said. "It didn't work."

BELOW:
Maurice Clarett sheds the tackle of Washington State's Erik Coleman in a fourth-quarter gain.
(Dispatch photo by Chris Russell)

RIGHT:
Buckeye receiver Michael Jenkins catches a 16-yard pass from Craig Krenzel against Cougar defender Marcus Trufant.
(Dispatch photo by Neal C. Lauron)

SATURDAY, SEPTEMBER 21, 2002

OHIO STATE 23 AT CINCINNATI 19

SURVIVING CINCINNATI

Bearcats can't convert in end zone as Buckeyes stay unbeaten

BY TIM MAY

Whoever coined the phrase "it's better to be lucky than good" hit the nail on the head. Just ask sixth-ranked Ohio State.

On the road against an in-state opponent for the first time since 1934, the Buckeyes were good when they absolutely had to be in escaping Cincinnati yesterday with a 23-19 win in Paul Brown Stadium. Quarterback Craig Krenzel's scrambling touchdown with 3:44 left provided the winning margin, and then a scrambling defensive stand against four Gino Guidugli

BELOW:
Ohio State quarterback Craig Krenzel lunges for the game winning touchdown in the fourth quarter. (Dispatch photo by Tim Revell)

passes to the end zone in the final minute provided the escape.

But on two of the passes from the OSU 15, receivers Jon Olinger, on first down, and George Murray, on third, had the ball in their hands only to drop it. On the last attempt, backpedaling linebacker Matt Wilhelm made a desperate leap at a slant pass intended for LaDaris Vann and popped it up, allowing safety Will Allen to intercept it in the back of the end zone.

With 26 seconds left, it finally was time for the undefeated Buckeyes (4-0) to take a deep breath. Against what was supposed to have been a 17-point underdog, the Buckeyes had a long day fraught with peril.

In front of what was announced as the largest crowd ever to see a football game in the Queen City (66,319), the teams battled on a day when whatever it took to win was the final motto. That included playing wide receiver Chris Gamble at defensive back at key junctures.

"We came out and got lucky, a little bit lucky," safety Mike Doss said.

Guidugli had a similar view.

"Twice I thought we had it won," said Guidugli, who was 26 of 52 passing for 324 yards, a TD and two interceptions.

It was Guidugli's play more than anyone else's that gave the Bearcats a chance at the end. He drove the Bearcats (1-2) from their 20 to the final firing point.

But after UC had taken a 12-7 lead to the half and regained the lead at 19-14 late in the third quarter, neither Guidugli nor coach Rick Minter wanted pats on the back for putting up the good fight.

"It sucks, it sucks so bad," Guidugli said. "We'd rather get blown out than lose like this."

Minter's summation: "We let an opportunity to win a big game get away. We made too many mistakes, too many errors in crunch time."

Up until then, Ohio State was the one making most of the errors. In the first half alone, the Buckeyes lost three turnovers—a fumble by Maurice Hall and the first two interceptions of the year thrown by

Krenzel—and had two big plays wiped out by penalties. The more serious was the holding call on the backside of what would have been a 96-yard TD kickoff return by Gamble after UC had upped its lead to 12-7 on Jonathan Ruffin's second field goal.

The only really good thing that had happened for the Buckeyes to that point was Krenzel's 20-yard pass to tight end Ben Hartsock for the first touchdown. But when Nate Salley stuck the Bearcats' Thaddeus Lewis at the UC 10 after the second-half opening kickoff, there was a detectable spark. A three-and-out defensive stand followed by a nine-yard punt return by Gamble to the UC 36 fueled the fire.

Running back Lydell Ross, who got the start for injured Maurice Clarett, then peeled off two runs for a total of 31 yards, followed by a rolling five-yard TD toss from Krenzel to Chris Vance. With 10:53 left in the third quarter, the Buckeyes had the lead for the first time, 14-12.

BELOW:
Buckeye back Lydell Ross bounces off the Bearcat defense after rushing for 18 yards in the second quarter.
(Dispatch photo by Neal C. Lauron)

	1st	2nd	3rd	4th	Final
OHIO STATE	0	7	7	9	23
CINCINNATI	9	3	7	0	19

SCORING SUMMARY

QTR	TEAM	PLAY		TIME
1st	**UC**	TD	McCleskey 1-yd. run (PAT fails)	10:13
1st	**UC**	FG	Ruffin 44-yd. field goal	6:24
2nd	**OSU**	TD	Hartsock 20-yd pass from Krenzel (Nugent kick)	10:03
2nd	**UC**	FG	Ruffin 49-yd. field goal	6:05
3rd	**OSU**	TD	Vance 5-yd. pass from Krenzel (Nugent kick)	10:53
3rd	**UC**	TD	Keith 5-yd. pass from Guidugli (Ruffin kick)	2:36
4th	**OSU**	FG	Nugent 24-yd. field goal	12:11
4th	**OSU**	TD	Krenzel 6-yd. run (2-pt. conv. fails)	3:44

——— OFFENSE ———

OHIO STATE

PASSING	ATT	COMP	YDS	INT	TD
Krenzel	29	14	129	2	2

RECEIVING	CATCHES	YDS	TD
Jenkins	5	47	0
Gamble	3	26	0
Hartsock	2	23	1
Vance	2	16	1
Ross	1	12	0
Carter	1	5	0

RUSHING	RUSHES	YDS	TD
Ross	23	130	0
Krenzel	9	26	1
Hall	3	7	0
Schnittker	1	1	0
Joe	1	1	0
TEAM	1	-2	0

CINCINNATI

PASSING	ATT	COMP	YDS	INT	TD
Guidugli	52	26	324	2	1

RECEIVING	CATCHES	YDS	TD
Keith	9	94	1
Vann	5	81	0
McCleskey	4	58	0
Olinger	3	55	0
Murray	2	13	0
Hart	1	14	0
Ross	1	6	0
Harwell	1	3	0

RUSHING	RUSHES	YDS	TD
McCleskey	13	69	1
Hall	1	16	0
Guidugli	6	6	0
Harwell	3	0	0

But the offense could not sustain the fire. Guidugli, feeding on a fourth and one stop of Ross by his defense moments earlier, led his team on an 11-play touchdown drive, his pass to Tye Keith gaining the final five yards and the lead, 19-14.

The Buckeyes countered with a long drive, and on fourth and two at the UC two, they elected to go for it. But after a timeout, they wound up with too many men on the field and were penalized. Mike Nugent came on for a 24-yard field goal to cut the lead to 19-17 with 12:31 left.

Guidugli then drove the Bearcats to the OSU 18. But on a first-down play from there, he and his receivers miscommunicated, and he lobbed a pass into the end zone that was intercepted by an all-alone Gamble.

OSU could not move the ball and punted, setting up the second biggest defensive play of the game. With UC at its 44, defensive end Darrion Scott rocked Guidugli and the ball popped free.

"It looked like a million dollars laying there," OSU defensive tackle David Thompson said. "So I jumped on it."

BELOW:
Cincinnati's Jamar Enzor sacks Ohio State quarterback Craig Krenzel for a loss of three yards in the first quarter. (Dispatch photo by Jeff Hinckley)

RIGHT:
With the pressure applied by Ohio State's E. J. Underwood, Cincinnati's Jon Olinger drops a pass on the first of Cincinnati's four failed attempts to score in the final seconds of the game. (Dispatch photo by Jeff Hinckley)

BELOW:
Ohio State's Will Allen celebrates his game-saving interception in the fourth quarter. (Dispatch photo by Tim Revell)

ABOVE:
Will Allen intercepts a Gino Guidugli pass to end the Bearcat run. Allen beat Bearcat LaDaris Vann (6). (Dispatch photo by Neal C. Lauron)

Ten plays later, including a 16-yard catch-and-run by Michael Jenkins and a six-yard gain by Ross—he wound up with 130 yards—on a third and one, Krenzel rolled left from the six and spun through a crowd of Bearcats into the end zone.

The Buckeyes rejoiced, but only for an instant. Guidugli and his teammates would deliver the final scare before it was over.

"We're very fortunate to leave Paul Brown Stadium with a win," coach Jim Tressel said. "But I'm awfully proud of the way our players kept playing and playing. That made the difference."

BY TIM MAY, THE COLUMBUS DISPATCH

MIKE DOSS

As far as Larry Doss is concerned, it didn't really matter who won the Thorpe Award, which goes annually to the nation's top defensive back.

"There's a lot of politics involved in those things," Doss said.

So when Terence Newman of Kansas State was named the 2002 winner on Dec. 12, ahead of Ohio State's Mike Doss, uncle Larry Doss took it in stride and told his nephew to do the same.

"I did feel bad for Mike not getting that award, because I really do believe he is the best defensive back in college football this year," Larry Doss said. "But that's not why he returned to Ohio State for his senior year.

"He came back to lead the Buckeyes to a national championship."

Larry Doss—Mike's legal guardian since Mike was eight—probably has a better handle on that than his nephew. He's witnessed firsthand Mike's "desire and determination" to rise above life's obstacles.

Last January, when Mike announced he wouldn't leave school a year early for the NFL, his uncle wasn't surprised.

"I definitely wanted him to stay, and I thought he would," Larry Doss said.

In Mike's mind, the decision came down to two noble pursuits: Leave, and he could afford to buy his mother, Diane Dixon, the house of her dreams. Stay, and he could help lead the Buckeyes toward a national championship that few folks thought was truly possible.

"We had told him, 'Your mom has been struggling for a long time, but her life has improved, and she'd probably want you to get that degree and enjoy one more year of college life,'" Larry Doss said. "We wanted him to maximize his college experience, and staying for his senior year would do that."

One last telephone conversation with his mom put Mike over the top on his decision to stay. Through tears, he announced it to the world, and he's been joyful ever since.

"Once you make the decision, that's it. You get on with your life," he said.

Diane Dixon refrains from interviews. But her smile seen after the Buckeyes capped their 13-0 regular season with a victory over Michigan on Nov. 23 told much of the story.

So did Mike's smile.

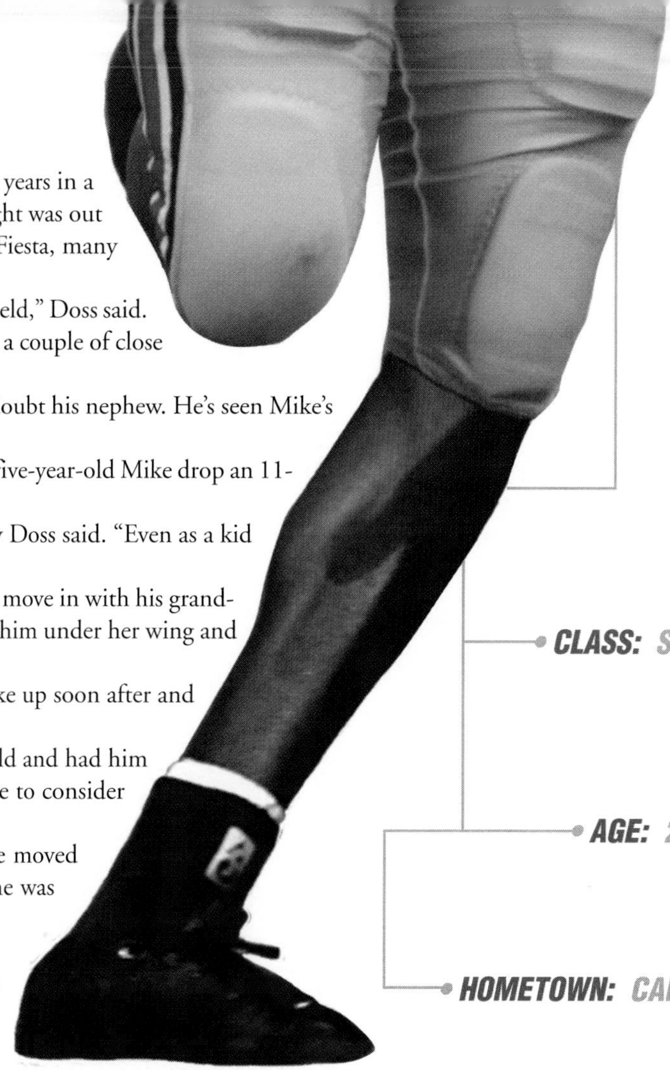

CLASS: SR.

AGE: 21

HOMETOWN: CANTON, OH

SAFETY

In becoming just the seventh OSU player in history to earn All-American honors three years in a row, he has improved his stock in the 2003 NFL draft and made good on a goal many thought was out of reach. When Doss said the team's aim was an unbeaten regular season and a spot in the Fiesta, many folks snickered.

"We were determined, we kept believing we could do it, and it showed out there on the field," Doss said. "And once the season got rolling, there were a couple of big wins here and there, and we had a couple of close ones."

Larry Doss wasn't sure what would happen this season, but he learned long ago not to doubt his nephew. He's seen Mike's physical and mental determination firsthand. For instance:

—In a pickup football game in the vacant lot next to his house in Canton, he watched a five-year-old Mike drop an 11-year-old with a blur of a tackle that left the older kid wincing.

"He's been fast and strong all of his life, and he always had a knack for the game," Larry Doss said. "Even as a kid he always liked to show off his muscles."

—A seven-year-old Mike, sensing he needed a change, walked four miles across town to move in with his grandmother Clara Doss and Larry. "It was his grandmother [who soon passed away] who tucked him under her wing and really got him started," Larry said.

Mike's father, Gene Doss, and Diane were teenagers when Mike came along. They broke up soon after and Gene moved to New York City.

Though he never missed a child support payment, visited with Mike as often as he could and had him up for visits, he didn't think New York was the right place to raise him. He had urged Mike to consider moving in with grandmother Clara and Larry. His mother encouraged it also, Larry said.

"Things really started working out for him after that," said Gene Doss, who has since moved back to Canton. "He started seeing how good he could be as a person. People found out he was really smart in school. He just settled in."

—Three times Mike hit winning home runs in youth baseball playoff games.

"Talk about an all-around athlete, he was probably a better baseball player than he was football; he was natural switch hitter, and as those home runs proved, he could rise to the occasion," Larry said. "But he became bored with baseball."

—During the football playoffs of his senior year at Canton McKinley, Mike made a key stop when the Bulldogs—gunning for their second straight state championship—faced one last desperation play from Cleveland St. Ignatius. Mike came all the way across the field to knock a receiver out of bounds with a vicious lick at the one-yard line.

"He was like a missile," said Larry, who claims that's still the signature Mike Doss football play. "No matter what, he was going to save the day."

Some would say Doss saved the day for Ohio State when he announced he was returning for his senior season.

"You couldn't dream anything better," Doss said of the 2002 season. "Coming back, I just wanted to be a team leader, and lead my guys out there and play with my class."

SATURDAY, SEPTEMBER 28, 2002

INDIANA 17 AT OHIO STATE 45

CLARETT RETURNS; ALL'S WELL

Freshman rushes for three TDs in win

BY TIM MAY

He's back.
If you have to ask who, you didn't pay attention to Ohio State's 45-17 win over Indiana yesterday in Ohio Stadium.

"Maurice the beast," OSU linebacker Cie Grant said.

Indeed, the player in question is freshman tailback Maurice Clarett, and Indiana coach Gerry DiNardo gave due credit after watching the Hoosiers fall to the sixth-ranked Buckeyes in the Big Ten opener for both teams.

BELOW:
Ohio State running back Maurice Clarett stiff-arms Indiana defender A. C. Carter on his way to a four-yard touchdown in the second quarter. (Dispatch photo by Mike Munden)

ABOVE:
Ohio State linebacker Matt Wilhelm brings down Indiana quarterback Gibran Hamdan on a fourth-and-three call in the fourth quarter. (Dispatch photo by Mike Munden)

"It's not like they don't have anybody else," DiNardo said. "But he's a good back. He's the real deal."

That's what folks were saying about Clarett before he underwent arthroscopic surgery on his right knee 12 days ago. It was obvious that Ohio State missed his physical running style eight days ago, when the Buckeyes pulled out a 23-19 win at Cincinnati.

But on the 50-yard drive for Ohio State's first touchdown yesterday, Clarett reasserted himself. In the 12-play march, he carried nine times for 33 yards and caught a pass for nine. Many of those yards were made with a lowered shoulder, carrying defenders with him. The culmination, a two-yard touchdown run, was proof that he was back.

"Somewhat," Clarett said. "Probably."

It's becoming Clarett's style to leave the glowing reviews to others, but after ripping off 104 yards rushing (giving him three 100-yard games in four starts as a collegian) and scoring three touchdowns (upping his season total to 10), there was no doubt about his impact.

"I think Maurice is starting to build that presence about himself," Grant said. "The opponents are thinking, 'Well, do we put nine in the box on him?' Then, when you can do what Craig Krenzel and those guys did today, spread it out and pass the ball, I think that's going to be even deadlier.

"But I think Maurice is developing a reputation. He runs hard. Anybody at the game knows this guy runs harder than any freshman I've ever seen."

Clarett tore the stitches in his right knee in the second quarter and had to have them redone so that he could play in the second half, when he gained 53 more yards before taking a seat.

"I try to be one of the toughest people on the team because people winning games have got to be tough," Clarett said. "If you saw Miami last year when they won the national championship, they were a tough team."

If people are talking about Ohio State in similar vein today, it's in large part because of Clarett. The Buckeyes (5-0) likely will climb to No. 5 in both major polls in the wake of fourth-ranked Florida State's loss at Louisville on Thursday.

But Clarett is the first to say that Ohio State, which will play at Northwestern on Saturday night, is not a one-man show. That was evident when Krenzel cranked up the passing attack, often from spread formations.

BELOW:
Buckeyes quarterback Craig Krenzel gains nine yards before Indiana's A. C. Carter takes him down in the third quarter.
(Dispatch photo by Fred Squillante)

	1st	2nd	3rd	4th	Final
INDIANA	0	10	0	7	17
OHIO STATE	7	14	17	7	45

SCORING SUMMARY

QTR	TEAM	PLAY		TIME
1st	**OSU**	TD	Clarett 2-yd. run (Nugent kick)	0:39
2nd	**IND**	FG	Robertson 49-yd. field goal	12:16
2nd	**OSU**	TD	Clarett 1-yd. run (Nugent kick)	5:42
2nd	**IND**	TD	Spencer 17-yd. pass from Hamdan (Robertson kick)	2:09
2nd	**OSU**	TD	Clarett 4-yd. run (Nugent kick)	0:38
3rd	**OSU**	TD	Gamble 43-yd. run (Nugent kick)	12:25
3rd	**OSU**	TD	Jenkins 4-yd. pass from Krenzel (Nugent kick)	6:38
3rd	**OSU**	FG	Nugent 51-yd. field goal	1:20
4th	**OSU**	TD	Jenkins 15-yd. pass from McMullen (Nugent kick)	5:43
4th	**IND**	TD	Roby 30-yd. pass from Jones (Robertson kick)	3:04

———— OFFENSE ————

INDIANA

PASSING	ATT	COMP	YDS	INT	TD
Hamdan	26	16	210	0	1
Jones	6	3	73	0	1

RECEIVING	CATCHES	YDS	TD
Roby	4	82	1
Johnson	4	50	0
Spencer	3	44	1
Pannozzo	2	44	0
Halterman	2	19	0
Washington	2	13	0
Anthony	1	21	0
Lewis	1	10	0

RUSHING	RUSHES	YDS	TD
Lewis	10	43	0
Washington	10	15	0
Haney	1	14	0
TEAM	1	-2	0
Hamdan	6	-14	0

OHIO STATE

PASSING	ATT	COMP	YDS	INT	TD
Krenzel	16	11	152	0	1
McMullen	7	7	65	0	1

RECEIVING	CATCHES	YDS	TD
Jenkins	7	93	2
Arden	3	36	0
Gamble	2	42	0
Vance	2	26	0
Ross	2	13	0
Clarett	1	8	0
McMullen	1	-1	0

RUSHING	RUSHES	YDS	TD
Clarett	21	104	3
Gamble	1	43	1
Hall	5	39	0
Nickey	1	28	0
Krenzel	5	15	0
Ross	2	11	0
Riley	2	11	0
McMullen	1	7	0
TEAM	1	-14	0

Krenzel was 11 of 16 for 152 yards. Michael Jenkins led the receivers with a season-high seven catches for 93 yards and two touchdowns—a four-yarder from Krenzel and a 15-yarder from backup Scott McMullen, both on fade patterns.

But Clarett's presence had the biggest impact, even on plays when he didn't touch the ball. He moved the Buckeyes from their 14-yard line to the Indiana 43 on four straight carries after the second-half kickoff. Krenzel then faked a handoff to Clarett and handed it to receiver Chris Gamble on an end-around. Gamble cut up the right sideline untouched to the end zone to push the Buckeyes' lead to 28-10.

LEFT:
Ohio State defenders Simon Fraser (75) and David Thompson (95) hit Indiana quarterback Gibran Hamdan, causing him to fumble the ball in the first quarter. The sack was good for a loss of three yards. (Dispatch photo by Neal C. Lauron)

BELOW:
Ohio State's Dustin Fox (37) blocks a third-quarter punt by Indiana's Ryan Hamre. (Dispatch photo by Mike Munden)

In the final analysis, Ohio State just had too much for the Hoosiers (2-3) in their first year under DiNardo. Ohio State's defense held them to 56 yards rushing and sacked quarterback Gibran Hamdan three times.

But Hamdan, who was 16 of 26 for 210 yards and one touchdown, was not the problem. He and the Hoosiers hung tough early and cut the OSU lead to 14-10 on a 17-yard touchdown pass to Tyke Spencer with 2:09 left in the first half.

But Gamble returned the ensuing kickoff 28 yards to the OSU 40, and the Buckeyes gained 15 more yards when he was pushed after going out of bounds. Krenzel then completed passes to Gamble, Jenkins and Chris Vance before Clarett swept around the right end for his third TD with 38 seconds left.

Indiana's fate was sealed early in the second half. Hamdan hit a wide-open Glenn Johnson on what likely would have been a 69-yard TD pass, but Johnson dropped the ball. Three plays later, Dustin Fox rushed in to block Ryan Hamre's punt, which rolled out of bounds at the Indiana 18. Krenzel soon found Jenkins on a four-yard pass, making it 35-10 with 6:38 left in the third quarter.

After Ohio State added a 51-yard field goal by Mike Nugent—pushing his field-goal streak to 10 in a row dating to last year at Michigan—Clarett retired for the day.

A week removed from the close call in Cincinnati, OSU's glow seemed to return.

"I think we're better than we were a week ago," coach Jim Tressel said. "But we're not where we want to be."

BELOW:
Ohio State coach Jim Tressel leads the team in "Carmen Ohio" at the end of the Indiana game. (Dispatch photo by Fred Squillante)

RIGHT:
Will Smith and Cie Grant celebrate after Smith broke up a pass by Indiana quarterback Gibran Hamdan, forcing a field goal in the second quarter. (Dispatch photo by Neal C. Lauron)

Ohio State's Lydell Ross runs for eight yards before Northwestern's John Pickens stops him in the second quarter. (Dispatch photo by Neal C. Lauron)

SATURDAY, OCTOBER 5, 2002

OHIO STATE 27 AT NORTHWESTERN 16

BUCKEYES BENT BUT NOT BROKEN

Clarett's fumbles just a part of OSU's close shave

BY TIM MAY

Maurice Clarett had a rocky start last night, but he made up for it before his rocky finish. Ohio State's freshman tailback lost three fumbles, including two in the first quarter that helped Northwestern take an early lead. But he rebounded to rush for 140 yards, score two touchdowns and help power the fifth-ranked Buckeyes to a surprisingly hard-fought 27-16 victory.

But Clarett's third lost fumble with 4:22 left in the game gave Northwestern—a 25-point underdog—one last legitimate gasp. Linebacker Cie Grant took care of that when he intercepted Brett Basanez with 3:33 left. It was Northwestern's first turnover.

BELOW:
The Ohio State defense puts the squeeze on Northwestern's Kunle Patrick in the fourth quarter.
(Dispatch photo by Mike Munden)

RIGHT:
Ohio State's Chris Gamble catches a 48-yard pass from Craig Krenzel to set up the Buckeyes' second touchdown. Northwestern's Marvin Ward made the stop.
(Dispatch photo by Chris Russell)

ABOVE:

Ohio State quarterback Craig Krenzel rushed for 23 yards in the first quarter. (Dispatch photo by Neal C. Lauron)

The Wildcats' second turnover came in the final minute when Dustin Fox separated tight end Eric Worley from the ball after a catch and Donnie Nickey recovered.

On a day when second-ranked Texas had a closer call than expected with Oklahoma State, the Buckeyes (6-0, 2-0) prevailed and emerged as the Big Ten's lone unbeaten team after Wisconsin's 31-28 loss to Penn State.

Along the way, OSU's Mike Nugent extended his consecutive field goal streak to 12—second longest in school history—with much-needed kicks of 41 and 30 yards in the second half.

But the glaring highlight of the night was the three lost fumbles by Clarett. He agreed.

"Horrible," Clarett said. "We won, though."

Clarett did do his part, one reason being that OSU coach Jim Tressel did not hesitate to put him back in the game.

	1st	2nd	3rd	4th	Final
OHIO STATE	0	14	10	3	27
NORTHWESTERN	6	3	7	0	16

SCORING SUMMARY

QTR	TEAM	PLAY		TIME
1st	**NU**	FG	Wasielewski 26-yd. field goal	7:25
1st	**NU**	FG	Wasielewski 27-yd. field goal	0:58
2nd	**OSU**	TD	Ross 3-yd. run (Nugent kick)	13:15
2nd	**NU**	FG	Wasielewski 37-yd. field goal	5:20
2nd	**OSU**	TD	Clarett 2-yd. run (Nugent kick)	2:43
3rd	**OSU**	FG	Nugent 41-yd. field goal	12:17
3rd	**OSU**	TD	Clarett 20-yd. run (Nugent kick)	6:33
3rd	**NU**	TD	Wright 9-yd. run (Wasielewski kick)	1:57
4th	**OSU**	FG	Nugent 30-yd. field goal	11:28

OFFENSE

OHIO STATE

PASSING	ATT	COMP	YDS	INT	TD
Krenzel	22	11	170	0	0

RECEIVING	CATCHES	YDS	TD
Jenkins	4	64	0
Gamble	2	51	0
Hartsock	2	26	0
Vance	1	13	0
Clarett	1	9	0
Carter	1	7	0

RUSHING	RUSHES	YDS	TD
Clarett	29	140	2
Ross	18	83	1
Krenzel	9	62	0

NORTHWESTERN

PASSING	ATT	COMP	YDS	INT	TD
Basanez	45	24	283	1	0

RECEIVING	CATCHES	YDS	TD
Patrick	6	63	0
Wright	4	37	0
Backes	4	32	0
Jordan	3	38	0
Philmore	3	20	0
Schweighardt	2	55	0
Worley	2	38	0

RUSHING	RUSHES	YDS	TD
Wright	24	95	1
Aikens	1	15	0
Basanez	1	2	0
Herron	1	1	0

"I've never been one that says a guy makes a mistake and he needs to sit and think about it for a month," Tressel said. "We've got to eliminate fumbles, though."

Clarett, the Big Ten's leading scorer going in, raised his season touchdown total to 12. The second leading rusher in the league going in, he pushed that total to 715 yards with his fourth 100-yards-plus game of the year.

But just as on the first road trip to Cincinnati two weeks ago, nothing came easy for the Buckeyes on a cool, clear night in front of 43,489 at Ryan Field. A tenacious Northwestern team (2-4, 0-2) saw to that.

BELOW:
Buckeyes fan Chad Combs cheers the team before Ohio State takes on Northwestern at Ryan Field.
(Dispatch photo by Chris Russell)

ABOVE:

Ohio State's Cie Grant tries to slip past Northwestern defenders after making an interception in the fourth quarter. Grant ran the ball back 23 yards. (Dispatch photo by Chris Russell)

"I'm disappointed for our kids, but I'm proud of our kids," Northwestern coach Randy Walker said. "There are critical plays in every game. Tonight, Ohio State made them and we didn't."

In terms of momentum, OSU defensive end Will Smith's play near the end of the first half was huge. With Northwestern facing third and goal at the one, Smith tipped a pass at the line and it flew harmlessly over everybody's heads.

Northwestern kicker David Wasielewski, who had hit three field goals earlier in the half, then missed right on an 18-yarder from the right hash mark. That allowed the Buckeyes—on the strength of a three-yard TD run by Lydell Ross and a two-yarder by Clarett—to go to the break with a 14-9 lead.

"To hold those guys to three field goals, I hope you could say we helped our team out," OSU safety Mike Doss said. "It gave our offense a little spark to say, 'The defense stepped up. Now it's our turn.' And they finally got going."

The OSU offense, sparked by a 56-yard return by Chris Gamble on the opening kickoff of the second half, scored on its first three possessions after the break. The Buckeyes had to settle for Nugent's 41-yard field goal after Gamble's return, but they drove 79 yards in 11 plays for Clarett's second TD—a 20-yard run around the right end—with 6:33 left in the third quarter for a 24-9 lead.

The second drive was kept alive by two third-down runs by quarterback Craig Krenzel, who along with hitting 11 of 22 passes for 170 yards and no interceptions also rushed for 62 yards on nine carries.

In between OSU's scoring drives in the third quarter, the Wildcats wasted a 67-yard kickoff return by Jason Wright when Wasielewski missed again, this time from 39 yards. But Basanez, who was 24 of 45 for 283 yards and one interception, and the Wildcats did not quit.

Following Clarett's second TD, Northwestern went on an 80-yard, nine-play drive capped by a nine-yard TD run by Jason Wright, who had 95 yards on 24 carries. That cut the OSU lead to 24-16 with 1:57 left in the third.

The Buckeyes answered with a 52-yard drive that resulted in Nugent's 30-yard field goal with 11:28 to play. They had been pushing for more when Ross, who had 83 yards on 18 carries, gained a first down to the seven. But dead-ball personal foul penalties against both teams left OSU with a first down at the 18. Three plays later, the Buckeyes settled for Nugent's 30-yarder.

OSU ended up with 455 total yards, 285 of that rushing, compared to Northwestern's pass-dominated 396 total yards.

"This win doesn't feel good, but it's a win, so you kind of take the good with the bad," Clarett said. "It doesn't feel like we're really 6-0 right now. It kind of feels like we're 4-2 because we could have played better.

"We played real, real bad tonight, but we still won."

35

MATT WILHELM

BY TIM MAY, THE COLUMBUS DISPATCH

CLASS: SR.

AGE: 21

L ike several players at Michigan and Ohio State, Matt Wilhelm had a choice. Growing up in Lorain, Ohio, and starring as a marauding linebacker at nearby Elyria Catholic High School, he was sought by both schools.

"I went to Michigan for the spring game before my senior year [in 1998], and Lloyd Carr offered me a scholarship on the field," Wilhelm said. "I told him, 'Give me seven days and I'll have an answer for you.'"

In the meantime, Wilhelm had a session with Fred Pagac, then Ohio State's defensive coordinator. Pagac's passion for all things OSU made the decision seem personal. It touched the right buttons with Wilhelm.

"The following Sunday I committed here to Ohio State, only because of coach Pagac and the overwhelming opportunity to play for the best team in the state in which you've lived your entire life," Wilhelm said.

Thus his die also was cast in The Game. He chose the side that, forever it seems, has been trying to play catch-up in one of college football's great rivalries. Michigan went 13-0-2 in the first 15 games in the rivalry and also has enjoyed an advantage of late, going 10-3-1 the last 14 years before this year's contest. But one of those three OSU victories came last year, in Jim Tressel's first season as coach. It came at Ann Arbor, on the same field where Carr had offered Wilhelm a scholarship, the same place where OSU hadn't won since 1987. It left Wilhelm with a sense that things have changed.

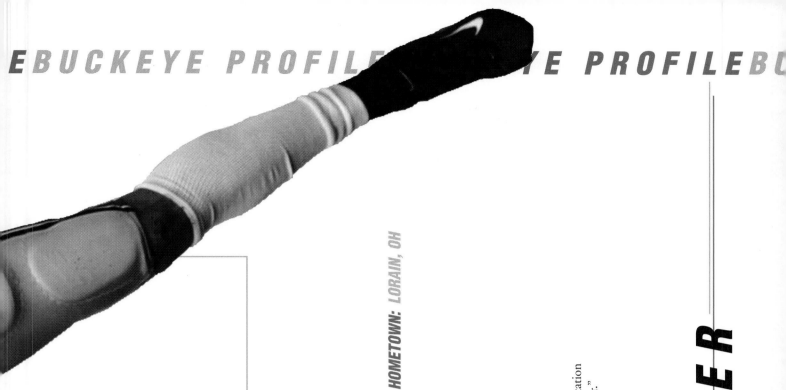

HOMETOWN: *LORAIN, OH*

LINEBACKER

"They've changed for the better," he said.

That was further in evidence when the Buckeyes outlasted the Wolverines 13-9 this year in Ohio Stadium, sending Ohio State to the Fiesta Bowl to play for the national championship.

Michigan had a knack for crashing similar OSU parties the past 10 years. The Buckeyes were handed their first loss of the season by Michigan in 1993, '95 and '96.

Back then, Wilhelm did not feel sympathy for OSU.

"If anything, I was a Notre Dame fan at that point, when they were in their glory years," he said. "But to lose those games the way we did, obviously is the reason why this is a big deal to the people of Columbus."

Wilhelm and the 12 other seniors on this OSU team will now be remembered for beating Michigan while the Buckeyes were on the doorstep of a national title. It will define their careers and certainly their final year.

It's fitting that Wilhelm, who had the best season of his college career at middle linebacker, will be so honored, because the year did not start auspiciously for Wilhelm. Rebounding from reconstructive surgery on his left ankle that forced him to miss spring ball, he didn't even start the first game against Texas Tech. But he quickly joined the fray and went on to become a Butkus Award semifinalist.

In a season of many key plays, Wilhelm had his share, including his fourth-down pass breakup in Week 4—in the shadow of his end zone—against Cincinnati that foiled the Bearcats' last chance for an upset.

His coach was confident that Wilhelm would be there in 2002, ankle surgery or not.

"Matt was not a concern about how he would come into this year," OSU coach Jim Tressel said.

And he finished the year with a flourish against Michigan.

"That's because great players should play great in great games," said former OSU linebacker Chris Spielman, who was part of two OSU wins over Michigan, in '84 and '87.

"You've got to play well in this game," Spielman said. "That's the reputation you want. I know it's the reputation Matt wants, because this game, especially, his last Michigan game, will live with him and his teammates forever."

As will the whole season.

SATURDAY, OCTOBER 12, 2002

SAN JOSE STATE 7 AT OHIO STATE 50

A HOMECOMING HIT

Fumble-forcing defense takes away any chance for upset

BY TIM MAY

Ohio State figured out a new way to do this homecoming thing.

After losing their previous two homecoming games, the Buckeyes dangled another possible thriller in front of a record Ohio Stadium crowd of 104,892 yesterday. Then they let linebacker Cie Grant go out and prove the big bang theory is real.

With 28-point underdog San Jose State threatening to make it a game, Grant's vicious lick on quarterback Scott Rislov caused a fumble that was scooped up by freshman Mike Kudla. It set in motion a perpetual turnover machine that led to fifth-ranked Ohio State's 50-7 blowout of the Spartans.

BELOW:

Ohio State's Cie Grant sacks San Jose State quarterback Scott Rislov and knocks the ball loose in the second quarter . OSU's Mike Kudla recovered the fumble and ran it back for 17 yards. (Dispatch photo by Neal C. Lauron)

"This was not a day when we could lose our focus," Grant said. "To get a nonconference game in the middle of the Big Ten season can be a distraction, but I thought we handled it very well."

The reward is expected to be an immediate uptick in the two major polls today after third-ranked Texas lost to second-ranked Oklahoma yesterday. But as Grant pointed out, there are still six games—all Big Ten games—left in the regular season for the Buckeyes (7-0), who must travel to Wisconsin on Saturday.

"What we've got to do is concentrate on what we can control, and that's how we play," Grant said.

In that regard, after Grant's hit, the Buckeyes were in total control yesterday in their first meeting with the Spartans (4-3). Consider:

—Quarterback Craig Krenzel and his receivers finally found the deep passing game they'd sought. Krenzel—11 of 14 for 241 yards and three touchdowns—connected with Michael Jenkins, Chris Vance and Chris Gamble on plays of 37 yards or more, the standout blows being a 37-yard TD pass to Vance in the second quarter and a 40-yarder to Jenkins in the third.

"A lot of that stemmed from the amount of time I had," Krenzel said. "Our O-line did a great job, and whenever you don't get touched back there it's pretty easy to go through your progressions and make the big plays."

ABOVE:
Ohio State's Chris Gamble catches a 47-yard pass from Craig Krenzel over San Jose State defender George T restin in the third quarter. (Dispatch photo by Fred Squillante)

> *THIS WAS A DAY WHEN WE COULD NOT LOSE OUR FOCUS. TO GET A NONCONFERENCE GAME IN THE MIDDLE OF THE BIG TEN SEASON CAN BE A DISTRACTION, BUT I THOUGHT WE HANDLED IT VERY WELL.*
>
> —BUCKEYE LINEBACKER CIE GRANT

	1st	2nd	3rd	4th	Final
SAN JOSE STATE	0	7	0	0	7
OHIO STATE	7	17	17	9	50

SCORING SUMMARY

QTR	TEAM	PLAY		TIME
1st	**OSU**	TD	Clarett 1-yd. run (Nugent kick)	9:39
2nd	**OSU**	FG	Nugent 36-yd. field goal	11:29
2nd	**SJS**	TD	Pauley 9-yd. pass from Rislov (Gilliam kick)	9:48
2nd	**OSU**	TD	Vance 37-yd. pass from Krenzel (Nugent kick)	8:40
2nd	**OSU**	TD	Clarett 5-yd. run (Nugent, Mike kick)	1:32
3rd	**OSU**	FG	Nugent 29-yd. field goal	11:49
3rd	**OSU**	TD	Clarett 7-yd. pass from Krenzel (Nugent kick)	9:51
3rd	**OSU**	TD	Jenkins 40-yd. pass from Krenzel (Nugent kick)	8:36
4th	**OSU**	TD	Ross 2-yd. run (Nugent kick failed)	13:37
4th	**OSU**	FG	Nugent 28-yd. field goal	9:52

OFFENSE

SAN JOSE STATE

PASSING	ATT	COMP	YDS	INT	TD
Rislov	44	36	265	0	1
Arroyo	5	0	0	0	0

RECEIVING	CATCHES	YDS	TD
Pauley	10	18	1
Broussard	9	69	0
Wooden	5	58	0
Starling	5	50	0
Ferguson	2	43	0
Walden	2	17	0
Helfman	2	4	0
Anderson	1	6	0

RUSHING	RUSHES	YDS	TD
Martin	5	12	0
Rigg	2	2	0
Staples	2	2	0
Ferguson	1	0	0
George	2	-2	0
Rislov	1	-14	0

OHIO STATE

PASSING	ATT	COMP	YDS	INT	TD
Krenzel	14	11	241	0	3
McMullen	9	8	114	0	0

RECEIVING	CATCHES	YDS	TD
Jenkins	7	136	1
Carter	4	76	0
Vance	2	51	1
Gamble	1	47	0
Hollins	1	14	0
Arden	1	14	0
Childress	1	9	0
Clarett	1	7	1
Ross	1	1	0

RUSHING	RUSHES	YDS	TD
Clarett	18	132	2
Ross	14	42	1
Hall	7	27	0
Parker	1	6	0
Riley	1	4	0
Krenzel	3	3	0
Otis	1	2	0
McMullen	1	-1	0
TEAM	3	-3	0

—Sophomore kicker Mike Nugent saw his point-after-touchdown streak stopped at 51 after a bad snap led to a miss. But he kicked three field goals (36-, 29- and 28-yarders) to push that streak to 15, tying Vlade Janakievski for the longest in school history.

—Freshman tailback Maurice Clarett, in the wake of his three-lost-fumbles game at Northwestern the week before, held onto the ball on all 18 of his carries for 132 yards, his fifth 100-plus game of the year. He also scored three touchdowns to push his Big Ten-leading season total to 15. His rushing total increased to 847.

—San Jose State had entered as the No. 1 team in the country in takeaways, but the Buckeyes were the ones who committed the thefts. They forced and recovered four fumbles, a season high. And they did it against a team that threw 49 passes and ran the ball only 13 times, netting zero yards on the ground.

ABOVE:
Ohio State's Donnie Nickey lofts the football he recovered after San Jose State's Jama Broussard fumbled in the third quarter.
(Dispatch photo by Neal C. Lauron)

"Last week at Northwestern you saw our guys flying around, giving up the yards, but giving the effort to get there and make the big hit," linebacker Matt Wilhelm said. "That's something we did again today."

Wilhelm had some of the bigger hits. They included one on San Jose State running back Trestin George on a fourth and one at the OSU 46 on the Spartans' first possession. He also caused a fumble deep in San Jose State territory midway through the third quarter with a lick on receiver Charles Pauley that set up Krenzel's seven-yard TD pass to Clarett.

But there was no debate on the hit of the game. Even as the Buckeyes built a 17-7 lead, San Jose State quarterback Scott Rislov had his spread offense clicking. He and the Spartans were content to peck away at OSU's defense with quick screens, outs and stop-route passes, and it took them to a first and goal at the OSU 10 with a little more than five minutes left in the first half.

As Rislov took the shotgun snap in the Spartans' five-receiver set, he looked left. Bearing down on him from the right was a blitzing Grant.

"I came through so clean and I thought, 'Oh, man, this guy does not see me coming,'" Grant said. "My whole intention was to try to punish him. That was the intention of the whole defense, punish the quarterback . . . It wears on him. And I think we did a great job of that."

On that play in particular.

"If we could have scored there it would have been a better situation for us," Rislov said. "It would have totally changed the momentum."

Kudla's 15-yard scoop-and-run added to the impact. Clarett's five-yard TD run eight plays later increased the OSU lead to 24-7 and started a landslide that buried the Spartans. On their next possession, linebacker Mike D'Andrea caused a fumble that was recovered by Dustin Fox just before the half. Then the Buckeyes scored on five of their first six possessions of the second half.

BELOW:
Ohio State's Lydell Ross gains six yards before getting tripped up by San Jose State's Melvin Cook in the first quarter.
(Dispatch photo by Fred Squillante)

RIGHT:
Ohio State's Simon Fraser (left) and Darrion Scott celebrate Scott's fumble recovery in the third quarter.
(Dispatch photo by Eric Albrecht)

Ohio State defenders Cie Grant (6), Mike Doss (2), Dustin Fox (37), and Robert Reynolds (44) gang tackle Wisconsin running back Anthony Davis. (Dispatch photo by Mike Munden)

SATURDAY, OCTOBER 19, 2002
OHIO STATE 19 AT WISCONSIN 14

PASSING A ROAD TEST

Fourth-quarter march lets Ohio State defeat Wisconsin, stay unbeaten

BY TIM MAY

This time, Ohio State's players did not dance on the midfield W at Camp Randall Stadium. They knelt and offered a prayer.

It was an appropriate prayer of thanks, said senior safety Mike Doss, who led the delegation after the fourth-ranked Buckeyes' 19-14 win over Wisconsin in a key Big Ten game in front of a chilled, frenzied crowd of 79,729.

To dance, as the Buckeyes did after they won on their last trip here in 2000, would have been a slap in

BELOW:
Ohio State's Cie Grant (left) and teammate Robert Reynolds wrap up Wisconsin's Anthony Davis in the second quarter.
(Dispatch photo by Neal C. Lauron)

ABOVE:

Ohio State receiver Michael Jenkins is taken down by Wisconsin's LaMarr Watkins (left) and B. J. Tucker after Jenkins made a long pass reception during the third quarter. (Dispatch photo by Mike Munden)

the face to the game they had just played, Doss said, and to the team they want to be.

"We're a different team here," Doss said. "Coach [Jim] Tressel says play and win with class. That's what it's all about."

As yesterday's game rolled into the fourth quarter with the Buckeyes trailing 14-13, though, it was all about getting out of town with the W.

"We knew it was going to be this kind of a football game, but we were just hoping to be the ones who had people step up and make the big plays," Tressel said.

That is what happened, Wisconsin coach Barry Alvarez said.

"They made a couple more plays than we did," Alvarez said.

Quarterback Craig Krenzel, receiver Michael Jenkins, tight end Ben Hartsock, receiver/cornerback

RIGHT:

Ohio State's Maurice Clarett is stopped by Wisconsin's LaMarr Watkins in the fourth quarter. (Dispatch photo by Mike Munden)

ABOVE:
Buckeyes quarterback Craig Krenzel steps back to pass in the first half against Wisconsin. Krenzel completed 12 of 19 pass attempts for 204 yards. (Dispatch photo by Doral Chenoweth III)

	1st	2nd	3rd	4th	Final
OHIO STATE	10	3	0	6	19
WISCONSIN	7	7	0	0	14

SCORING SUMMARY

QTR	TEAM	PLAY		TIME
1st	**OSU**	TD	Jenkins 47-yd. pass from Krenzel (Nugent kick)	13:30
1st	**WIS**	TD	Davis 41-yd. run (Allen kick)	5:49
1st	**OSU**	FG	Nugent 27-yd. field goal	2:48
2nd	**OSU**	FG	Nugent 25-yd. field goal	13:14
2nd	**WIS**	TD	Orr 42-yd. pass from Sorgi (Allen kick)	1:55
4th	**OSU**	TD	Hartsock 3-yd. pass from Krenzel (2-pt. conv. fails)	9:59

——— OFFENSE ———

OHIO STATE

PASSING	ATT	COMP	YDS	INT	TD
Krenzel	19	12	204	0	2

RECEIVING	CATCHES	YDS	TD
Jenkins	5	114	1
Gamble	3	65	0
Hartsock	3	13	1
Schnittker	1	12	0

RUSHING	RUSHES	YDS	TD
Clarett	30	133	0
Krenzel	10	24	0
Ross	3	18	0
Gamble	1	3	0

WISCONSIN

PASSING	ATT	COMP	YDS	INT	TD
Sorgi	15	7	137	1	1
Bollinger	3	3	21	0	0
Daniels	1	1	2	0	0

RECEIVING	CATCHES	YDS	TD
Orr	4	107	1
Charles	3	30	0
Williams	2	16	0
Bernstein	1	5	0
Bollinger	1	2	0

RUSHING	RUSHES	YDS	TD
Davis	25	144	1
Smith	7	41	0
Sorgi	3	8	0
Bernstein	2	8	0
Bollinger	6	-10	0
Morse	1	-11	0

Chris Gamble, tailback Maurice Clarett, kicker Mike Nugent, punter Andy Groom—they topped the list of those who stepped forward and helped the Buckeyes (8-0, 3-0) keep alive their quest for a berth in the national championship game.

But there were two plays on which the game pivoted:

—Play No. 1 involved Krenzel and Jenkins, who had hooked up on a 47-yard touchdown pass on the game's third snap. It was that combination that clicked again with the game in the balance in the fourth quarter. On a third and six from the OSU 16, Jenkins went up to take away a 45-yard pass from two Wisconsin defenders.

Krenzel, after keeping the drive alive moments later with a scrambling third-down 16-yard run down the right sideline to the Wisconsin 15, found tight end Ben Hartsock wide open on a three-yard touchdown pass that capped the 88-yard, nine-play march and gave

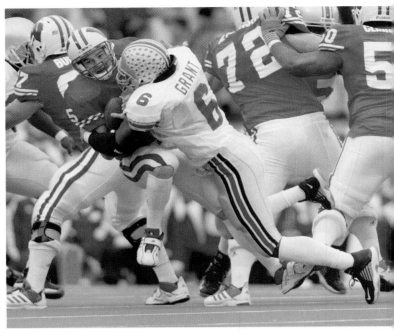

ABOVE:
Ohio State's Cie Grant sacks Wisconsin quarterback Brooks Bollinger in the second quarter. Bollinger was sacked on the next play and left the game with a concussion.
(Dispatch photo by Neal C. Lauron)

BELOW:
Buckeye receiver Michael Jenkins makes a move on the Badgers' B. J. Tucker after catching a Craig Krenzel pass. Jenkins scored on the play, a 47-yard reception.
(Dispatch photo by Mike Munden)

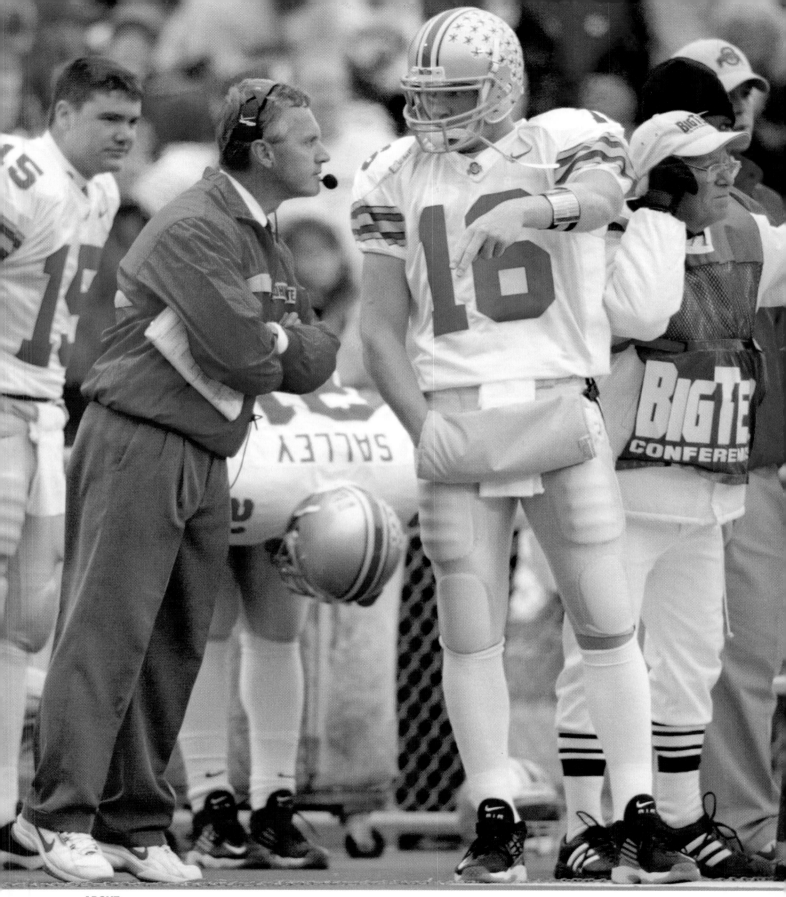

ABOVE:
Buckeyes quarterback Craig Krenzel confers with head coach Jim Tressel on the sidelines during the Wisconsin game at Camp Randall Stadium. (Dispatch photo by Mike Munden)

the Buckeyes the lead. The pass attempt for two failed, but what mattered most was what happened next.

—Play No. 2 involved Gamble. Wisconsin backup quarterback Jim Sorgi, who took over after Brooks Bollinger had to leave with a concussion, had given the Badgers the 14-13 lead with a 42-yard pass to Jonathan Orr with 1:55 left in the first half.

When the Badgers needed a big play near the end, it was no surprise that Sorgi looked for Orr again, especially when they looked up and saw Gamble as the coverage man.

"They saw a wide receiver out there, and I guess they thought, 'Let's go at him,'" Gamble said.

What the Badgers (5-3, 0-3) hadn't seen, evidently, was Gamble's fourth-quarter interception that helped save the day in the Buckeyes' other close call this year, the 23-19 win at Cincinnati. Sorgi lofted a fade route toward the goal line. Gamble, running with Orr all the way, beat him to the ball for the interception, falling into the left part of the end zone for a touchback with 7:09 left.

When OSU could not gain a first down, it put Groom on the big-play spot. He already had held for Nugent's field goals of 27 and 25 yards in the first half that extended Nugent's school-record streak to 17 and,

in the final analysis, provided the difference on the scoreboard.

But Groom had to deliver on his specialty. He launched his longest punt this year, a 74-yarder that rode to the Wisconsin end zone.

Then it was up to the OSU defense again.

"Anthony Davis had more than 100 yards rushing at halftime, the first back to go over 100 on us this year," said Doss, who led OSU with a season-high 14 tackles. "We just took that as a personal challenge to our defense to hopefully step up and make some plays.

"To shut that team out in the second half, that showed we keep working hard every play."

Never more so than after Groom's punt. Davis wound up with 144 yards, but he gained only one yard on first down as Tim Anderson, Gamble and others ran him down. Sorgi missed on a second-down pass and had a third-down toss intended for Orr broken up by Dustin Fox. The Badgers punted.

Up stepped Clarett with 4:29 left. The freshman, on his way to 133 yards, already had notched his sixth 100-yard game of the year, though he didn't score a touchdown for the first time in the seven games he's played. But after that punt, his two carries to a first down and two more to set up Krenzel for a sneak to another first down ensured the Buckeyes would be able to run out the clock.

"When the game was on the line we made the plays," said Krenzel, who finished 12 of 19 for 204 yards and his seventh no-interception game of the year. "Our defense did a great job of shutting them out when they needed to.

"I think we showed today we're a tough team, and you've got to play 60 minutes if you want to beat the Buckeyes."

BELOW:
Ohio State's Maurice Clarett tries to break away from Wisconsin's Broderick Williams in the first half.
(Dispatch photo by Doral Chenoweth III)

RIGHT:
OSU's Ben Hartsock celebrates with teammates Redgie Arden and Ryan Hamby (80) after Hartsock scored the go-ahead touchdown in the fourth quarter. (Dispatch photo by Doral Chenoweth III)

7

CHRIS GAMBLE

BY TODD JONES, THE COLUMBUS DISPATCH

CLASS: SO.

AGE: 19

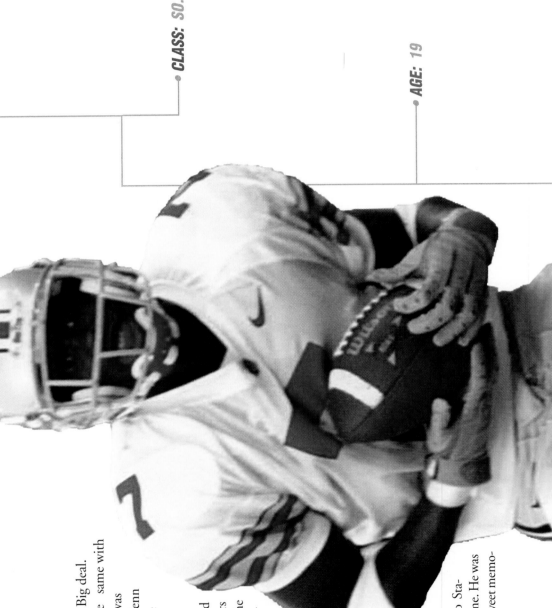

So they've cloned sheep. Big deal. Ohio State has done the same with a football player, and it was evident Oct. 26 when Penn State suffered through the horror film forever known as The Three Faces of Gamble.

The star's name is Chris Gamble, and if the NCAA ever decides to pay players (yeah, right), it'll need to compensate the OSU sophomore for overtime. He certainly earned it in the Buckeyes' 13-7 win over Penn State.

Gamble, a Sunrise, Fla., native, performed his usual roles as offensive receiver and punt returner. He also made his first start at cornerback and played the entire game on defense. No wonder he said he got into the whirlpool before the game began.

When the game ended, the Ohio Stadium crowd was chanting Gamble's name. He was grass-stained and limping, but he had sweet memories to soothe his ache.

Chief among them was his third-quarter interception that he returned 40 yards for a touchdown, on one of those Looney Tunes-type of darts.

At the time, his interception gave the flanker—hey, that's what he's listed at—a team-high three for the season, and he nearly had another, batting down a Zack Mills pass with one arm. Gamble also caught one pass (for minus one yard) and returned five punts for 64 yards.

"I was cramping up a lot on defense in the second half," he said. Never did Gamble consider leaving the game. OSU linebacker Matt Wilhelm didn't realize his teammate was hurting until Gamble told him before Penn State's final offensive play.

"I was going to carry him off the field," Wilhelm said. The OSU coaches might want to carry Gamble on their shoulders for saving the Buckeyes at a thin position.

"We really didn't expect to play him as much [at corner] as we did," defensive coordinator Mark Dantonio said. "He was playing well. We asked him if he wanted a break, and he said no."

Gamble had practiced 30 minutes at cornerback all week. That was enough to convince OSU coach Jim Tressel. He consulted with Dantonio and defensive backs coach Mel Tucker, and they decided the Thursday before the game to start Gamble on defense. He was told that Friday.

"He deserved to be seen and noted by the whole country as a two-way starter," Tressel said. "A lot of talented guys in this world don't have a feel for the game. He has a feel for the game."

Gamble said he knew all of OSU's coverages, helped by hand signals from safeties Michael Doss and Donnie Nickey. His interception came in a three-deep zone.

Just as important as his TD was his first-quarter tackle of Penn State's Anwar Phillips, who had run 58 yards with a recovery of a fumble by OSU quarterback Craig Krenzel and appeared to be en route to a TD.

"I had him run down and wanted to swat the ball out of his hands and make him fumble," Gamble said.

As if he hadn't done enough.

"He's unbelievable—Deion Sanders back there," OSU linebacker A. J. Hawk said.

The game was a sign of things to come.

Gamble started—and often starred—at both receiver and cornerback in the Buckeyes' last four games.

HOMETOWN: SUNRISE, FL

RECEIVER/CORNERBACK

PENN STATE 7 AT OHIO STATE 13

GAMBLE PAYS OFF

Two-way star helps OSU defense put clamps on PSU

BY TIM MAY

In the biggest game of the year to date, Ohio State's defense ruled Penn State yesterday, and Chris Gamble—the first player to start both ways for the Buckeyes in what school officials said was 39 years—was its king.

A regular at wide receiver, Gamble also started at cornerback yesterday. With the Buckeyes trailing early in the third quarter, he picked off a Zack Mills pass and zigzagged 40 yards untouched to fourth-ranked Ohio State's only touchdown in the 13-7 victory over No. 18 Penn State.

BELOW:
Ohio State linebacker A. J. Hawk sacks Penn State quarterback Zack Mills in the third quarter. (Dispatch photo by Chris Russell)

ABOVE:

Buckeye tailback Lydell Ross runs through an opening in the Penn State defense in the third quarter. Ross ran for 40 yards and caught passes for 30 yards in the game. (Dispatch photo by Chris Russell)

"I saw the ball in the air and I attacked it," Gamble said.

That pretty much summed up not only his day but that of the OSU defense, as it made up for a season-high four turnovers by the offense by corralling three of its own. They were all interceptions of Mills, who had victimized the Buckeyes (9-0, 4-0) by rallying the Nittany Lions (5-3, 2-3) from an 18-point deficit to win at Penn State a year ago.

But this time, even as the OSU offense kept dropping the rabbit, there would be no magic for Mills or running back Larry Johnson. Buoyed by an Ohio Stadium-record crowd of 105,103, the defense turned

RIGHT:

A. J. Hawk grabs a pass intended for Penn State's Matt Schmitt (right) in the first quarter. Hawk ran the interception back for 10 yards. (Dispatch photo by Barth Falkenberg)

in its best effort of the season, limiting the Nittany Lions to 81 yards rushing and 98 passing.

"They met a defense that was on a mission," OSU coach Jim Tressel said.

Penn State's Joe Paterno, the winningest major-college coach in history, concurred.

"We couldn't make a play when we had to," Paterno said. "We couldn't come up with a catch, or Zack was a little off. A couple of times we had some running room and we got tripped up.

"It's a lot of little things, and [Ohio State] is a good football team. That is a very good defensive football team."

The Buckeyes kept pace with Iowa—the teams don't play this year—in the Big Ten race, after the Hawkeyes won big at Michigan. Ohio State also stayed viable in the Bowl Championship Series race, in which it was ranked sixth in the first official standings last week.

ABOVE:
Ohio State's Maurice Hall gets taken down by Penn State's Gino Capone (47) and teammate Rich Gardner (25) in the second quarter. Hall gained 16 yards and a first down on the play.
(Dispatch photo by Neal C. Lauron)

BELOW:
Ohio State's Chris Gamble intercepts a Zack Mills pass and begins his 40-yard runback for a touchdown in the third quarter.
(Chris Russell/Dispatch Photo)

	1st	2nd	3rd	4th	Final
PENN STATE	7	0	0	0	7
OHIO STATE	0	3	10	0	13

SCORING SUMMARY

QTR	TEAM	PLAY			TIME
1st	**PSU**	TD	Johnson 5-yd. run (Gould kick)		0:36
2nd	**OSU**	FG	Nugent 37-yd. field goal		6:16
3rd	**OSU**	TD	Gamble 40-yd. interception return (Nugent kick)		13:07
3rd	**OSU**	FG	Nugent 37-yd. field goal		1:05

——— OFFENSE ———

PENN STATE

PASSING	ATT	COMP	YDS	INT	TD
Mills	28	14	98	3	0

RECEIVING	CATCHES	YDS	TD
Johnson, L.	6	32	0
Smith	2	25	0
Lukac	2	18	0
Johnson, T.	2	14	0
Johnson, B.	1	6	0
Robinson	1	3	0

RUSHING	RUSHES	YDS	TD
Johnson, L.	16	66	1
Robinson	2	8	0
Mills	5	7	0

OHIO STATE

PASSING	ATT	COMP	YDS	INT	TD
Krenzel	20	13	112	2	0

RECEIVING	CATCHES	YDS	TD
Jenkins	3	34	0
Ross	3	30	0
Hartsock	3	29	0
Hall	2	15	0
Vance	1	5	0
Gamble	1	-1	0

RUSHING	RUSHES	YDS	TD
Ross	21	40	0
Krenzel	15	39	0
Clarett	4	39	0
Hall	8	20	0
Gamble	1	3	0

How much the win over the Nittany Lions will help OSU in the BCS standings won't be clear until Monday. But in the self-esteem category, it was huge.

Considering that the Buckeyes went into the game without right tackle Shane Olivea (appendectomy) and wound up losing freshman tailback Maurice Clarett (shoulder injury) after his third carry did not bode well for the offense. Before leaving, Clarett had gained 39 yards on four carries to become only the second freshman in OSU history to top 1,000 (1,017), joining Robert Smith (1,126 in 1990).

But quarterback Craig Krenzel took the Buckeyes to the PSU one on that first drive before losing a fumble that PSU's Anwar Phillips returned 58 yards. It was a harbinger, though, that Gamble was the one who ran down Phillips.

Penn State had only one drive of significance, just before the end of the first quarter. Mills and Johnson took the Nittany Lions 80 yards in nine plays. Johnson took an option pitch around the right end five yards for the score.

After that, the OSU defense tightened the screws.

The OSU offense, on the other hand, never could gain a consistent grip. It did keep the ball for 37:29 of the 60 minutes, a major feat considering the turnovers.

"On offense, it wasn't as much about what they did to us as it was what we did to us," Krenzel said.

Kicker Mike Nugent stayed solid, pushing his school-record field-goals-made streak to 19, starting with a 37-yarder with 6:16 left in the first half and including another 37-yarder that kissed the right upright to push OSU's advantage to 13-7 some 12 minutes after Gamble's TD.

But that the OSU offense also blew some opportunities was obvious. For example, receiver Chris Vance fumbled away a pass at the Penn State 14 late in the first half.

And it was Krenzel who gave Penn State one last real chance when, midway through the fourth quarter and from the PSU 40, he tossed an interception to the Lions' Shawn Mayer, the ball winding up at midfield. But the defense again rose and forced a punt.

BELOW:
Buckeye quarterback Craig Krenzel eludes Penn State's Michael Haynes in the third quarter. (Dispatch photo by Chris Russell)

ABOVE:

Buckeye tailback Maurice Clarett runs for 30 yards on his first carry against the Penn State Nittany Lions in the first quarter.
(Dispatch photo by Neal C. Lauron)

The bad news for OSU was that it was downed at the six. Four plays later, that's where the Big Ten's leading punter, Andy Groom, had to work from, and he delivered a 59-yarder. A clipping call against Penn State on the long return pushed it back to the 20.

The defense forced a three and out, but again, even starting from its 42, the OSU offense was assaulted by PSU defensive tackle Jimmy Kennedy and his buddies. Groom was asked for an encore. He banged a 55-yarder from the OSU 34, Bobby Britton made a shoestring tackle of return man Bryant Johnson at the

15, and then the defense did its thing again.

That Gamble got away with an obvious pass interference on Penn State's final play from scrimmage was a sign that things were going right for the defense—and for him.

"It feels good to contribute," said Gamble, who now has three interceptions, all of them playing huge in the Buckeyes' run. "That's all I want to do out there, is make plays and try to help us win any way I can."

He and the Buckeyes found a way yesterday, and now, at 9-0, that's what mattered most.

100

Ohio State's Maurice Clarett reacts after time ran out in the fourth quarter and the Buckeyes defeated Penn State. Clarett was injured on Ohio State's first series and did not return to the game. (Dispatch photo by Tim Revell)

SATURDAY, NOVEMBER 2, 2002

MINNESOTA 3 AT OHIO STATE 34

OSU DEFENSE HAS ITS WAY

Buckeyes top Golden Gophers 34-3 in front of 104,897 Ohio Stadium fans

BY TIM MAY

In any preseason discussion about Ohio State's prospects for the season, there were obvious questions.

Would the offense come around behind a rebuilt offensive line and new starting quarterback Craig Krenzel? Would freshman Maurice Clarett live up to his billing and supplant sophomores Lydell Ross and Maurice Hall at tailback? Would sophomore kicker Mike Nugent be able to make more than 50 percent of his field goal attempts?

BELOW:
Ohio State's Michael Jenkins slips by Minnesota's Eli Ward (27) after making a reception in the second quarter. Jenkins gained 49 yards to set up a Lydell Ross touchdown. (Dispatch photo by Mike Munden)

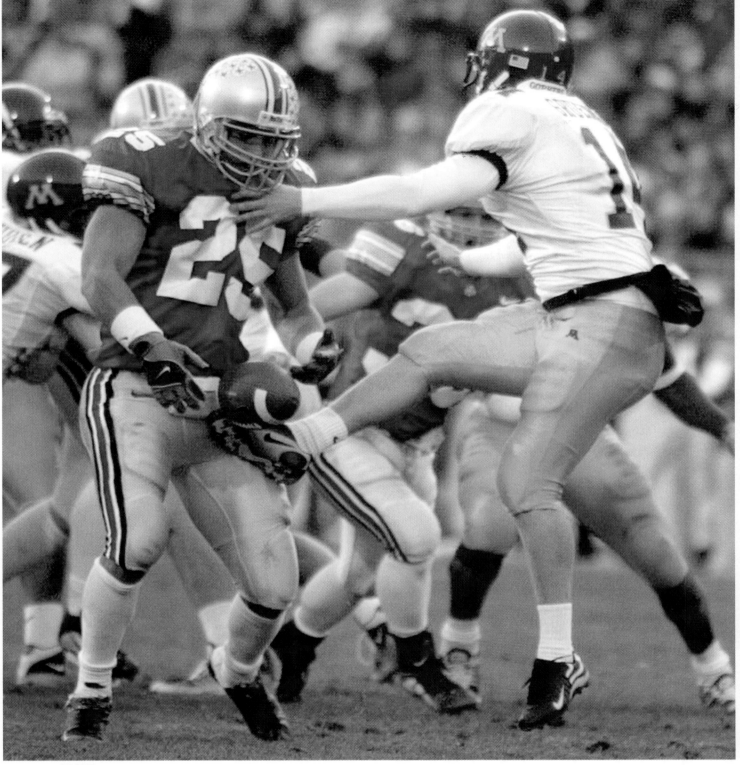

ABOVE:
Ohio State's Donnie Nickey (25) blocks a punt by Minnesota's Preston Bruening in the second quarter. Nickey recovered the block at the Minnesota 14-yard line. (Dispatch photo by Mike Munden)

But defense? It was a given. The last three games have proved that, with the exclamation point being sixth-ranked Ohio State's 34-3 win over 23rd-ranked Minnesota yesterday before 104,897 in Ohio Stadium.

While the OSU offense struggled to find a pace early with Clarett benched because of lingering effects from a shoulder injury, the defense dominated.

Whether Minnesota (7-2, 3-2) would have scored had the Gophers not converted on a 24-yard field goal after they blocked an Andy Groom punt on OSU's first possession is up to conjecture. But the Gophers netted 53 yards rushing and 59 passing. They entered the game No. 3 in the Big Ten in total offense with a 441.4-yard average.

In the meantime, the OSU offense found the spark it needed in a familiar way—a long pass play from Krenzel to Michael Jenkins. Then the running game started to pick up steam with Ross (89 yards on 20 carries, two touchdowns) and Hall (93 yards on 14 carries, one TD) slowly finding a rhythm.

Along the way, Nugent kicked two more field goals to push his school-record streak to 21.

But there was no doubt that with the game in the balance, Ohio State's defense did the real kicking.

"They've carried us the past two weeks," Krenzel said, referring to the 13-7 win last week over Penn State. "The offense came out a little slow again today and the defense kept us in the game. Obviously, last week the defense won the game for us. These past couple-three games they have been playing awesome for us.

"That's the kind of thing we need to keep happening for the next three games for us to be where we want to be."

The aim of the Buckeyes (10-0, 5-0) is still on the grand prize—a berth in the Fiesta Bowl—and they believe their only shot is to win out. In that race, they saw Notre Dame, Georgia, Virginia Tech and North Carolina State fall to the wayside yesterday.

In the Buckeyes' same sights, though, is the Big Ten championship. That clearly has turned into a two-team race with Iowa (9-1, 6-0), which kept rolling with a 20-3 win over Wisconsin yesterday.

That means despite becoming only the seventh team in OSU history to be 10-0, the Buckeyes have little time to celebrate. Upcoming are two straight road games, at Purdue and Illinois, followed by the regular-season finale at home with Michigan.

"But that's definitely a momentum plus for your team, knowing you're 10-0 now," defensive end Darrion Scott said. "We've got a lot of momentum going into the next game, we've got a shot to be 11-0."

BELOW:
Ohio State's Tim Anderson takes down Minnesota quarterback Asad Abdul-Khaliq in the first quarter.
(Dispatch photo by Karl Kuntz)

	1st	2nd	3rd	4th	Final
MINNESOTA	3	0	0	0	3
OHIO STATE	0	10	17	7	34

SCORING SUMMARY

QTR	TEAM	PLAY		TIME
1st	**Minnesota**	FG	Nystrom 24-yd. field goal	10:05
2nd	**OSU**	TD	Ross 5-yd. run (Nugent kick)	5:59
2nd	**OSU**	FG	Nugent 37-yd. field goal	3:31
3rd	**OSU**	TD	Ross 9-yd. run (Nugent kick)	12:35
3rd	**OSU**	FG	Nugent 33-yd. field goal	5:25
3rd	**OSU**	TD	Vance 30-yd. pass from Krenzel (Nugent kick)	1:15
4th	**OSU**	TD	Hall 4-yd. run (Nugent kick)	6:29

——— OFFENSE ———

MINNESOTA

PASSING	ATT	COMP	YDS	INT	TD
Abdul-Khaliq	20	10	59	0	0

RECEIVING	CATCHES	YDS	TD
Hosack	3	25	0
Burns	3	16	0
Baugus	2	10	0
Mays	2	8	0

RUSHING	RUSHES	YDS	TD
Jackson	16	49	0
Tapeh	8	32	0
TEAM	1	-13	0
Abdul-Khaliq	11	-15	0

OHIO STATE

PASSING	ATT	COMP	YDS	INT	TD
Krenzel	15	9	128	0	1
McMullen	1	1	16	0	0

RECEIVING	CATCHES	YDS	TD
Gamble	3	15	0
Jenkins	2	62	0
Hartsock	2	4	0
Vance	1	30	1
Childress	1	17	0
Carter	1	16	0

RUSHING	RUSHES	YDS	TD
Hall	14	93	1
Ross	20	89	2
Riley	7	26	0
TEAM	1	-3	0
Krenzel	8	-11	0
Groom	1	-16	0

"When you see on the scoreboard one of the teams ahead of us [Notre Dame] lose, you get excited. There's a lot of things that get us going right now."

What really got the whole team involved yesterday was a Krenzel-to-Jenkins reception midway through the second quarter. The 49-yard catch-and-run by Jenkins ended at the Minnesota five. On the next play, Ross ripped through the middle for the touchdown, giving the Buckeyes the lead for good at 7-3 with 5:59 left in the first half.

OSU safety Donnie Nickey followed with a tit-for-tat special teams blow, racing in untouched to block a Jason Gruening punt and falling on it at the Minnesota 14. When the offense went backward, Nugent hit from 37 yards to push the lead to 10-3.

The landslide, almost imperceptible at first, had begun. Going back to the first TD, the Buckeyes scored on five straight possessions, helped along the way by several Minnesota errors. The biggest came when Gruening, trying to corral a wide snap on Minnesota's fourth play of the second half, fell to the ground at his nine. Two plays later, Ross started left, then cut behind a wall of blockers and lunged for the end zone for a nine-yard touchdown that upped the OSU lead to 17-3.

By all rights, the game could have been called by technical knockout at that point because the OSU defense gave up just seven yards to Minnesota in the second half. Tailback Terry Jackson, the Big Ten's leading rusher going in with a 128.8-yard average, was checked at 49 yards on 16 carries. Running-passing quarterback Asad Abdul-Khaliq could do little of either, completing 10 of 20 passes but getting sacked four times, including another spectacular planting by Scott. The sacks helped result in his minus-15 yards rushing on 11 carries.

It led to a blowout by appearance, Minnesota coach Glen Mason said, but not by definition.

"The perception will be, because they put 34 points on the board, we didn't play good defense. I don't think that's really true," Mason said.

The fact that Ohio State's defense ruled the day again, though, was a given.

BELOW:
Ohio State's Lydell Ross tiptoes beyond the reach of Minnesota's Justin Isom on his way to a 26-yard gain in the first quarter. Ross ran for 89 yards in the win. (Dispatch photo by Neal C. Lauron)

RIGHT:
Ohio State's Maurice Hall carries the ball late in the second quarter. Minnesota's Justin Fraley (12) and Ken Williams (13) take him down. (Dispatch photo by Doral Chenoweth III)

LEFT:
Ohio State quarterback Craig Krenzel is sacked for a loss of seven yards by Paul Nixon in the first quarter. (Dispatch photo by Mike Munden)

BELOW:
With help from Kenny Peterson (97) and Tim Anderson (54), Ohio State's Simon Fraser sacks Minnesota quarterback Asad Abdul-Khaliq for a loss of three yards in the first quarter. (Dispatch photo by Neal C. Lauron)

RIGHT:
Chris Vance points skyward after scoring the third quarter touchdown. (Dispatch photo by Doral Chenoweth III)

85

CLASS: SO.

BY AARON PORTZLINE AND ROB OLLER, THE COLUMBUS DISPATCH

MIKE NUGENT

The indecision was killing Mike Nugent's kicking.

Last season, the freshman from Centerville would wait nervously on the sideline while the Ohio State coaches discussed which kicker should attempt a field goal—Nugent or Josh Huston.

"I feel real calm this year," Nugent said after kicking field goals of 40, 33 and 45 yards during the 51-17 win Sept. 8 over Kent State. "I'm not waiting at fourth down where they have to make a decision right there who is going to kick. I know if we've got the ball on the 50-yard line and get stopped I'm going to be the guy to go in there."

Of course, Nugent blames himself for making it difficult for coaches to rely on him in 2001, when he made only seven of 14 field goal attempts and the Buckeyes' kicking game was an exercise in brutality.

"I'd get in my own head last year," he said. "I'd say, 'Shoot, the grass is a little bad where I'm kicking.' Now I've got my head on straight."

It showed this season. Counting his last kick in the 2001 season, Nugent set an Ohio State record by making 24 field goals in a row—he finally missed from 37 yards out against Illinois on Nov. 16—and finished the year 24 of 26. His FG streak shattered

AGE: 20

HOMETOWN: CENTERVILLE, OH

KICKER

the OSU record and came up only one shy of the national mark set by Chuck Nelson of Washington in 1982. He also made 41 of 42 point-after-touchdown kicks.

Nugent's exploits earn him recognition as a finalist for the Lou Groza Award and, along with those of senior punter Andy Groom, gave the Buckeyes a huge advantage over most opponents.

While decisiveness from the coaches played a part in Nugent's improvement, so may have a stroll he took across Ohio State's campus in the summer. Nugent walked by coach Jim Tressel's camp for high-school students, noticed that St. Louis Rams kicker Jeff Wilkins was among the instructors, and struck up a conversation that has turned into a friendship.

"I asked him if we could hang out a little while, and we did," Nugent said. "I spent a couple of days working with him, and it was just incredible for me from a confidence standpoint. I mean, who has dealt with more pressure in the last few seasons than the place-kicker for the St. Louis Rams? He's played in two Super Bowls.

"The whole thing about kicking is you can go out and have three or four good games and then fall apart," he said. "So the biggest thing is consistency.

"On the sidelines you want to know that the guys are behind you, but a lot of the times the kicker is off on his own," Nugent said. "Now, I've got the guys telling me I'm going to put it right down the middle. They're behind me and I'm feeling good about it."

So is the coaching staff.

"I've quit dwelling on last year," offensive coordinator Jim Bollman said. "He's obviously had some tough experiences the past couple of years, and he's learned from it and he's a lot better for it now."

Tressel said Nugent's confidence is apparent even in practice.

"If it's not straight down the middle, if it's even a little bit to the left, he's not happy with it," Tressel said. "He wants perfection, and that's good."

"I'm just relaxing and kicking through the ball and trusting myself and my ability," Nugent said. "Before I was over-thinking everything. I'd worry about the wind and the snap and how everything was going to go. Now it's just me, my foot and the ball, and it's going great."

SATURDAY, NOVEMBER 9, 2002

OHIO STATE 10 AT PURDUE 6

HARD-BOILED WIN FOR OSU

Jenkins's TD catch with 1:36 left saves Buckeyes from falling

BY TIM MAY

The measure of a true heavyweight contender is one that can take a beating yet somehow summon a late uppercut to save the day.

On an afternoon when top-ranked Oklahoma couldn't find that desperate punch at Texas A&M, third-ranked Ohio State did against Purdue to stay alive in the national championship race.

A bruised and battered OSU offense took everything the Purdue defense could fire at it for 58 minutes. Then quarterback Craig Krenzel and receiver

BELOW:
Ohio State's Matt Wilhelm grabs Purdue quarterback Brandon Kirsch and drags him down for a loss of six yards in the fourth quarter. The Buckeye defense held the Boilermakers to a field goal on the series. (Dispatch photo by Eric Albrecht)

RIGHT:
Ohio State receiver Michael Jenkins makes the go-ahead touchdown reception over Purdue's Antwaun Rogers in the fourth quarter. The Buckeyes came from behind to beat the Boilermakers 10-6. (Dispatch photo by Neal C. Lauron)

Michael Jenkins stepped up and delivered a haymaker that sent the Boilermakers reeling 10-6 in a classic Big Ten fight yesterday in front of 65,250 fans in windswept Ross-Ade Stadium.

If the Buckeyes wind up in the Fiesta Bowl on Jan. 3 to battle for the national championship—they are one step closer thanks to Oklahoma's 30-26 loss—Krenzel's 37-yard touchdown pass to Jenkins on fourth and one with 1:36 left will be a big reason why. Chris Gamble's leaping interception (his fourth of the season) sealed the deal with 45 seconds left.

"It feels like we're almost kind of destined," Jenkins said. "We've been playing hard. It's been rough on the road. We've needed to pull games out.

"We've just got to take two more games and see what happens in the end."

The next stop for OSU (11-0, 6-0) is at Illinois on Saturday before a return home Nov. 23 to host Michigan in the season finale.

The Buckeyes, second in the Bowl Championship Series ratings last week behind Oklahoma and ahead of defending champion Miami, no doubt will maintain a top two spot when the BCS ratings are released Monday afternoon. But that wasn't the immediate concern of coach Jim Tressel, even though OSU moved to 11-0 for the first time since 1995.

"We're not going to drop in the Big Ten standings," he said, as the Buckeyes kept pace with Iowa. "That's what is most important."

BELOW:
Buckeye quarterback Craig Krenzel slips out of the tackle of Purdue's Niko Koutouvides on his way to 15 yards in the second quarter. Krenzel rushed 12 times for 39 yards. (Dispatch photo by Neal C. Lauron)

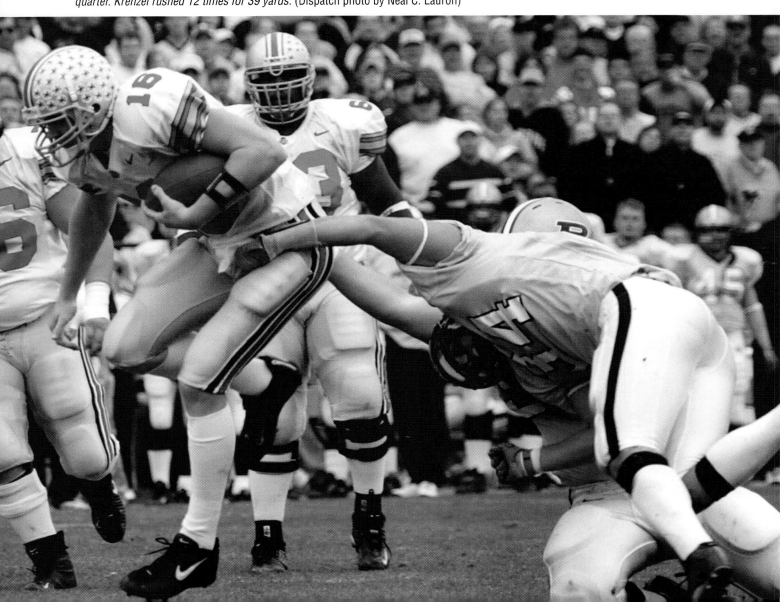

	1st	2nd	3rd	4th	Final
OHIO STATE	0	3	0	7	10
PURDUE	3	0	0	3	6

SCORING SUMMARY

QTR	TEAM	PLAY		TIME
1st	**Purdue**	FG	Lacevic 21-yd. field goal	0:42
2nd	**OSU**	FG	Nugent 22-yd. field goal	0:00
4th	**Purdue**	FG	Lacevic 32-yd. field goal	7:50
4th	**OSU**	TD	Jenkins 37-yd. pass from Krenzel (Nugent kick)	1:36

———— OFFENSE ————

OHIO STATE

PASSING	ATT	COMP	YDS	INT	TD
Krenzel	20	13	173	1	1

RECEIVING	CATCHES	YDS	TD
Jenkins	5	87	1
Gamble	3	5	0
Hartsock	2	21	0
Ross	1	8	0
Childress	1	7	0
Clarett	1	-1	0

RUSHING	RUSHES	YDS	TD
Clarett	14	52	0
Ross	11	24	0
Krenzel	12	19	0
Hall	1	1	0
TEAM	1	-2	0

PURDUE

PASSING	ATT	COMP	YDS	INT	TD
Orton	28	18	169	3	0
Kirsch	11	9	116	0	0

RECEIVING	CATCHES	YDS	TD
Standeford	8	57	0
Stubblefield	7	63	0
Chambers	7	44	0
Harris	2	45	0
Williams	1	58	0
Rhinehart	1	9	0
Jones	1	9	0

RUSHING	RUSHES	YDS	TD
Jones	12	28	0
Harris	11	25	0
Void	1	2	0
Kirsch	5	1	0

Once again the Buckeyes can thank their defense, which extended its stranglehold on opponents that began in the second half at Wisconsin four games ago. Yet it was one slip by that defense that put the Buckeyes in serious jeopardy against a Purdue team (4-6, 2-4) desperate for a victory.

Ohio State had contained Purdue starting quarterback Kyle Orton and his halftime reliever, Brandon Kirsch, for three quarters, but Kirsch hit a wide-open Ray Williams on a 58-yard pass behind a busted deep coverage.

For some observers, it must have summoned memories of Ohio State's last trip here in 2000, when Drew Brees found a wide-open Seth Morales for a 67-yard touchdown pass with 1:55 left that beat the Buckeyes 31-27.

This time, Purdue didn't score on the big play, which was stopped by safety Donnie Nickey at the Ohio State 22-yard line. The Boilermakers pushed the ball to the five, but blitzing linebacker Matt Wilhelm sacked Kirsch on third down. That forced the Boilermakers to settle for a 32-yard field goal from Berin Lacevic that gave them a 6-3 lead with 7:50 left.

The Boilermakers must have felt like they had the Buckeyes right where they wanted them, considering the inconsistent play of the OSU offense all day and that any charge had to be mounted into a 15 mph wind. The first drive fizzled at the Purdue 49, but the Buckeyes countered with a punt from Andy Groom that was downed at the eight and was followed by a three-and-out stand by the defense, forcing Purdue to punt.

Ohio State's Dustin Fox intercepts a pass intended for Purdue's John Standeford (82) in the first quarter.
(Dispatch photo by Neal C. Lauron)

ABOVE:

Buckeye tailback Maurice Clarett is held to a one-yard gain by Purdue's Niko Koutouvides (34) and Brandon Johnson (90) in the second quarter. Clarett rushed for 56 yards for the day. (Dispatch photo by Eric Albrecht)

Brent Slaton banged it 57 yards, but Gamble returned it 22 yards to the Purdue 46. There was 3:10 left and a sense that it was Ohio State's last shot. That became painfully obvious when a pass from Krenzel to tight end Ben Hartsock on third and 14 from the 50 gained only 13 yards.

With the running game—hurt by the early exit once again of freshman tailback Maurice Clarett (shoulder stinger)—having been stuffed at key points all day, the Buckeyes went to the line intent on throwing the ball for the first down. Krenzel's first choice was to Hartsock, but he was covered. Then he looked for Jenkins, who was running a takeoff route with one-on-one coverage by Antwaun Rogers. Krenzel stepped up and fired a rainbow into the wind that found its way to Jenkins at the goal line.

Several other key factors also stand out.

The Buckeyes, after a diving Wilhelm interception at the Purdue 41, had to scramble for a Mike Nugent field goal on the last play of the first half, his 21st field goal of the year without a miss. Krenzel was stopped at the four on the previous play with 12 seconds left, but the field goal unit ran onto the field quickly and got the snap off with one second left.

And there was the way the defense, even though it gave up 285 yards passing, made most of the plays that mattered, including getting the ball back for one last shot at the end.

The long pass to victory seemed poetic justice for what Purdue did here two years ago, but OSU safety Mike Doss—victimized then, but he led the team with nine tackles yesterday—said memories had nothing to do with it.

"We weren't even thinking about two years ago, man, this is 2002," Doss said. "We've got guys working hard week in and week out. That's all we can do. It's a 60-minute game, we kept fighting, we got some breaks near the end.

"Big-time players make big plays, and that's what our guys did."

RIGHT:

Ohio State's Craig Krenzel (16) runs for a yard as Purdue's Landon Johnson and Niko Koutouvides stop him in the second quarter. (Dispatch photo by Eric Albrecht)

LEFT:

Ohio State's Ben Hartsock (88) makes a 13-yard reception over Purdue's Antwaun Rogers in the fourth quarter. This play set up the 37-yard touchdown reception by Jenkins that gave the Buckeyes the victory. (Dispatch photo by Neal C. Lauron)

BELOW:

Ohio State's Matt Wilhelm celebrates with Buckeyes fans at the end of the game at Ross-Ade Stadium in West Lafayette, In. Wilhelm was credited with eight tackles in the Buckeyes' win. (Dispatch photo by Eric Albrecht)

Ohio State's Adrien Clarke (63) leads a prayer at midfield in a crowded Ross-Ade Stadium after the Buckeyes came from behind to beat Purdue. (Dispatch photo by Neal C. Lauron)

CRAIG KRENZEL 16

BY TIM MAY, THE COLUMBUS DISPATCH

It's a good thing Craig Krenzel has proved to be a winning quarterback; he'd probably have no future as a lyricist.

That was proved in late November when the Ohio State band stopped by to serenade the Buckeyes as part of the buildup for the 99th renewal of The Game with Michigan. As tight end Ben Hartsock recalled, the group was really getting into "We don't give a damn for the whole state of Michigan" when Krenzel spoke up.

"I think we should add an asterisk to that song," he said. "It should be, 'We don't give a damn for the whole state of Michigan except for where Krenzel's from.'"

Hartsock laughed. Clearly, that would throw off the meter. But it is true that Krenzel, of Utica, is the only Michigander on the Ohio State roster. And don't think Michigan fans haven't noticed.

"I've seen the hate mail he's getting from guys from Michigan," OSU safety Donnie Nickey said. "We were laughing at one. I can't tell you what it said. This is a family show.

"But it's hate mail. He's not intimidated by it. It was immature, poorly written. We were kind of making fun of the guy who wrote it."

It's not surprising some folks up north are upset. Not only did he bolt the state, but in his first start as a collegian last year, Krenzel—playing for a benched Steve Bellisari—kept his cool and led the Buckeyes to their first win in Michigan Stadium since 1987.

But if an asterisk is to be added, it should be based on what Krenzel did this season. Seen as a fill-in whom the fans hoped wouldn't mess things up a year ago, Krenzel was one of the major reasons Ohio State advanced to the national championship game in the Fiesta Bowl.

QUARTERBACK

CLASS: JR.

AGE: 21

HOMETOWN: UTICA, MI

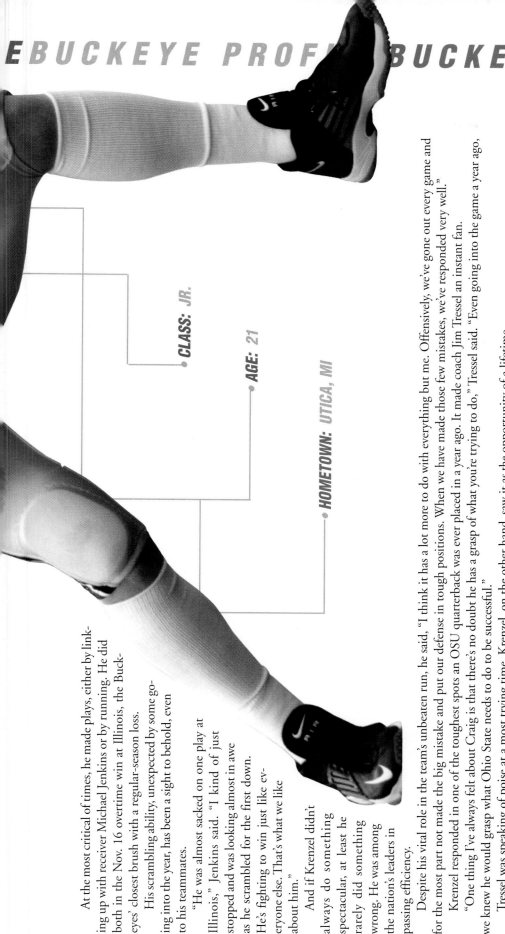

At the most critical of times, he made plays, either by linking up with receiver Michael Jenkins or by running. He did both in the Nov. 16 overtime win at Illinois, the Buckeyes' closest brush with a regular-season loss.

His scrambling ability, unexpected by some going into the year, has been a sight to behold, even to his teammates.

"He was almost sacked on one play at Illinois," Jenkins said. "I kind of just stopped and was looking almost in awe as he scrambled for the first down. He's fighting to win just like everyone else. That's what we like about him."

And if Krenzel didn't always do something spectacular, at least he rarely did something wrong. He was among the nation's leaders in passing efficiency.

Despite his vital role in the team's unbeaten run, he said, "I think it has a lot more to do with everything but me. Offensively, we've gone out every game and for the most part not made the big mistake and put our defense in tough positions. When we have made those few mistakes, we've responded very well."

Krenzel responded in one of the toughest spots an OSU quarterback was ever placed in a year ago. It made coach Jim Tressel an instant fan.

"One thing I've always felt about Craig is that there's no doubt he has a grasp of what you're trying to do," Tressel said. "Even going into the game a year ago, we knew he would grasp what Ohio State needs to do to be successful."

Tressel was speaking of poise at a most trying time. Krenzel, on the other hand, saw it as the opportunity of a lifetime. "I was excited," he recalled.

"Surprisingly, I wasn't that nervous. I had a lot of confidence in our team that they were going to play well and kind of rally around me and make sure it wasn't going to be up to me to win the football game, which is what happened."

There has been a different dynamic this year, especially when the OSU offense had to redefine itself when freshman tailback Maurice Clarett became an on-again, off-again player after suffering a shoulder injury midway through the season. The Buckeyes leaned on Krenzel often down the stretch.

"I've always prided myself on being able to control my emotions and take care of the task at hand," Krenzel said.

The Buckeyes will back him, even if he is from Michigan.

"We never gave him any crap about being from Michigan," Nickey said. "He came to us, to Ohio State, so we're not going to knock him for that.

"Once you're here, you're a Buckeye . . . I'm glad we stole him."

OHIO STATE 23 AT ILLINOIS 16

FOR OSU, IT'S 12 AND OH!

First-ever OT game fails to derail Buckeyes as they hold off Illinois

BY TIM MAY

Yesterday, Ohio State moved to a realm where it has never been, 12-0, and to get there it had to survive a predicament in which had never been, overtime.

But then, what did you expect? The Buckeyes, living this great season—they're No. 1 in the Bowl Championship Series ratings—in which they've played average at best on the road, stayed true to form against Illinois in windswept, cold Memorial Stadium. They gave up a tying 48-yard field goal to John Gockman on

BELOW:
Ohio State quarterback Craig Krenzel (16) runs for a series-saving first down during overtime. (Dispatch photo by Mike Munden)

the last play of regulation, then made an eight-yard touchdown run by Maurice Hall in the first period of overtime stand up for a 23-16 win.

"The most important thing is the way we hung in there as a team," OSU defensive tackle Tim Anderson said. "We could have given up there towards the end, but we kept fighting. I think that's the most important thing that came out of today."

It turned out that way after he and linebacker Cie Grant bull-rushed Illinois quarterback Jon Beutjer with the Illini facing fourth and eight at the nine on what turned out to be the last play. Beutjer tried to fire a pass toward Aaron Moorehead, who was slanting from the right.

"I just stuck my arms up and hoped for the best," Anderson said.

The ball struck his left forearm and dropped to the ground. In an instant, the game was over, Ohio State's unbeaten season was still alive, and thoughts turned almost immediately to the regular-season finale against archrival Michigan in Ohio Stadium.

Perhaps the most crucial thing is that the game is not on the road, where OSU won five trips this season by a combined 31 points.

"Nobody said it was going to be easy, playing on the road, trying to win a Big Ten championship," said OSU receiver Michael Jenkins, who again led the team with six catches for 147 yards, including a 50-yard TD catch. "We just stuck together and played 60 minutes—65 minutes tonight—and were able to pull out wins on the road."

Escaping with a win was the most important thing about yesterday, OSU coach Jim Tressel said. As for whether No. 12 meant something special to him, he said "No."

BELOW:
Ohio State's Mike Nugent misses a field goal wide left, his first miss this season, in the first half. (Dispatch photo by Mike Munden)

	1st	2nd	3rd	4th	OT	Final
OHIO STATE	6	0	7	3	7	23
ILLINOIS	0	3	10	3	0	16

SCORING SUMMARY

QTR	TEAM	PLAY		TIME
1st	OSU	FG	Nugent 33-yd. field goal	7:13
1st	OSU	FG	Nugent 47-yd. field goal	2:31
2nd	Illinois	FG	Gockman 40-yd. field goal	0:31
3rd	Illinois	TD	Young 19-yd. pass from Beutjer (Christofilakos kick)	13:13
3rd	OSU	TD	Jenkins 50-yd. pass from Krenzel (Nugent kick)	12:00
3rd	Illinois	FG	Gockman 47-yd. field goal	2:55
4th	OSU	FG	Nugent 37-yd. field goal	14:14
4th	Illinois	FG	Gockman 48-yd. field goal	0:00
OT	OSU	TD	Hall 8-yd. run (Nugent kick)	15:00

——— OFFENSE ———

OHIO STATE

PASSING	ATT	COMP	YDS	INT	TD
Krenzel	21	10	176	0	1

RECEIVING	CATCHES	YDS	TD
Jenkins	6	147	1
Gamble	1	14	0
Vance	1	9	0
Hall	1	3	0
Hartsock	1	3	0

RUSHING	RUSHES	YDS	TD
Hall	17	69	1
Ross	15	51	0
Krenzel	12	26	0
TEAM	1	-1	0

ILLINOIS

PASSING	ATT	COMP	YDS	INT	TD
Beutjer	45	27	305	0	1
TEAM	1	0	0	0	0

RECEIVING	CATCHES	YDS	TD
Young	10	144	1
Moorehead	4	48	0
Lloyd	4	33	0
Harris	3	22	0
Lewis	2	32	0
McClellan	2	17	0
Davis, C.	1	5	0
Davis, J.	1	4	0

RUSHING	RUSHES	YDS	TD
Harris	21	62	0
Davis, C.	3	7	0
Beutjer	10	-16	0

That's because even at 12-0, the Buckeyes have won nothing. Yesterday, Iowa (11-1, 8-0), which OSU does not play, clinched at least a share of the Big Ten title with a regular-season-ending win at Minnesota.

Throw in the fact that the Buckeyes can't afford a loss at this point if they want to play in the Fiesta Bowl national championship game Jan. 3 and it adds up to one of the more pressurized Michigan games ever.

Or to put it in calmer terms, "As long as we keep winning, we're going to be where we want to be," Jenkins said.

Tressel had warned that Illinois—the defending Big Ten champ and a team that had won three of its last four games after losing five of its first six—was playing its best of the season.

Thus when OSU could muster only two field goals from Mike Nugent in the first half, despite starting or ending its first five possessions in Illinois territory, the battle was on. That signal was sent by Gockman hitting a 40-yard field goal near halftime to cut OSU's lead to 6-3.

Buoyed by a 52-yard punt return from Eugene Wilson early in the third quarter, the Illini moved quickly to a 10-6 lead as Beutjer tossed a 19-yard TD pass to Walter Young over the head of Dustin Fox.

But on the Buckeyes' next possession, quarterback Craig Krenzel and Jenkins worked magic similar to what they had in the last two minutes at Purdue a week earlier. Krenzel laid a rainbow into the hands of Jenkins to push OSU back into the lead at 13-10 with 12 minutes left in the third quarter.

Beutjer and the Illini found a way to nitpick down the field against OSU's vaunted defense, then settled for a 47-yard field goal into the wind by Gockman with 2:55 left in the third quarter, tying the score at 13. Ohio State responded immediately by moving to a 37-yarder from Nugent, also into the wind.

BELOW:
Ohio State's head coach Jim Tressel organizes his offense during the game against Illinois. (Dispatch photo by Mike Munden)

Nugent had missed his first kick of the season from almost that same spot in the second quarter, snapping his school-record streak at 23. He missed again from 41 yards with 5:31 left in the game, giving Illinois hope.

That hope seemed to vanish, though, when Gockman came up five yards short on a 59-yard field goal attempt with 2:17 left. Except the Illini defense turned around and stoned a once again inconsistent OSU offense, forcing a punt at 1:04.

Beutjer pushed his team from its 25 to the OSU 31 in seven plays, completing four passes, including a seven-yarder to Greg Lewis on a fourth and five. Gockman then delivered to send the game into overtime.

Krenzel's 14-yard scramble on third and 10 from the 25 in OT helped save the day, and then Hall scored behind a crushing block from Adrien Clarke.

After gaining a first at the 11, followed by a three-yard run, Beutjer saw a fade to Moorehead get caught just out of bounds, and a fade to Young, behind Chris Gamble, be ruled a bobble by an official. Then came the final play, Anderson's block.

ABOVE:
Ohio State's Matt Wilhelm upends Illinois running back Antoineo Harris for a loss in the first quarter. (Dispatch photo by Neal C. Lauron)

ABOVE:
Ohio State's Lydell Ross (30) is stopped by the Illinois defense. The Buckeyes were close to a touchdown, only to be pushed back by penalties. They ended up with only a field goal. (Dispatch photo by Neal C. Lauron)

SATURDAY, NOVEMBER 23, 2002

MICHIGAN 9 AT OHIO STATE 14

HOME FREE
FOR TEMPE

Clutch plays drive Ohio State to victory over Michigan, into national-title game

BY TIM MAY

As dusk settled over Ohio Stadium yesterday, the goal posts were still standing and so was the Ohio State football team. They'd all stood up to supreme tests.

The second-ranked Buckeyes capped a regular-season stretch run that qualified them for membership in the drama club with a pulse-pounding 14-9 win over Michigan in front of the largest crowd—105,539—in stadium history.

Thousands stormed the field to join in a celebration that included pats on the back, player rides on fans' shoulders and an assault on the south goal posts that finally was quelled by pepper spray from the authorities.

BELOW:
Ohio State fullback Brandon Schnittker makes a 15-yard reception for a first down to keep the winning drive alive in the final minutes. (Dispatch photo by Eric Albrecht)

The jubilation, though, will go on indefinitely. With freshman Maurice Clarett giving the offense the lift it needed, with Maurice Hall scoring the winning touchdown with 4:55 to play, and with the defense forcing turnovers on Michigan's last two possessions—Will Allen's interception at the two ended the game—the Buckeyes stayed perfect.

They rose to a plateau—13-0—the school has never reached before, and now they're headed to a game in which no Big Ten team has ever played. Immediately after, with their Big Ten cochampionship trophy already on display, they were invited by Fiesta Bowl officials to play in the Bowl Championship Series national title game on Jan. 3.

"We accept," coach Jim Tressel said.

Whether there are some who still question the Buckeyes' credentials at this point is moot.

"Ohio State did everything it needed to do to find a way to win," Michigan coach Lloyd Carr said.

All OSU needs now is a Fiesta Bowl opponent, which likely won't be known until at least Dec. 7.

"We said before the season we want to finish 13-0 and we want to win the national championship game," junior quarterback Craig Krenzel said. "We have an opportunity to do that, and we just have to go out, work hard and get better."

ABOVE:
Ohio State's A. J. Hawk (47) and teammate Mike Doss (2) stop Michigan's B. J. Askew for a loss during the second half. (Dispatch photo by Neal C. Lauron)

Yesterday, the Buckeyes stayed true to form. The defense was big when it had to be and the offense, buoyed by the return of Clarett and the no-mistake play of Krenzel, delivered just enough. It added up to a second straight win over Michigan, the first time OSU

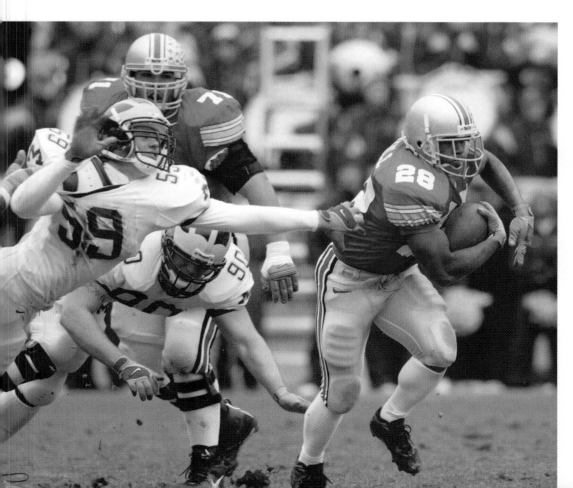

LEFT:
Ohio State's Maurice Hall slips out of the reach of Michigan's Joey Sarantos (59) on his way to a long gain in the third quarter. A holding call negated the play. (Dispatch photo by Neal C. Lauron)

has done that since 1981 and '82 in a series which Michigan leads 56-37-6, and in which it had won 12 of the previous 17.

"Like Jonathan Wells said last year [after the Buckeyes' first win at Michigan since 1987], this is definitely a rivalry," said OSU senior linebacker Matt Wilhelm, who was in on a game-high 15 tackles for the Buckeyes, two more than senior safety Mike Doss. "I think we brought some of that swagger back."

What stood out down the stretch, he said, was the way the team fought to the final play. And so it was again yesterday.

Hall raced three yards around the right end off an option pitch from Krenzel for the go-ahead TD. It capped an eight-play, 57-yard drive that featured Krenzel sneaking one yard to the Michigan 32 on fourth and one and hitting a wide-open Clarett with a 26-yard pass on the following play to the six.

Clarett, who did not play at Illinois last week as the coaches opted to rest his sore left shoulder, vowed to play yesterday "because it's the Michigan game. It's all that matters to this point." He wound up with 119 yards on 20 carries, pushing his season mark to 1,190 to top the OSU freshman rushing record of 1,126 yards set by Robert Smith in 1990.

Clarett's entry in the first quarter provided an obvious lift to the offense and the crowd. More than that, it provided the power to OSU's only other scoring drive, a 10-play, 76-yarder that he capped with a two-

BELOW:
Michigan's Marlin Jackson leaves his feet to tackle Ohio State's Maurice Clarett after Clarett gained 18 yards in the fourth quarter.
(Dispatch photo by Karl Kuntz)

	1st	2nd	3rd	4th	Final
MICHIGAN	3	6	0	0	9
OHIO STATE	7	0	0	7	14

SCORING SUMMARY

QTR	TEAM	PLAY		TIME
1st	**Michigan**	FG	Finley 36-yd. field goal	8:35
1st	**OSU**	TD	Clarett 2-yd. run (Nugent kick)	2:56
2nd	**Michigan**	FG	Finley 35-yd. field goal	10:56
2nd	**Michigan**	FG	Finley 22-yd. field goal	0:16
4th	**OSU**	TD	Hall 3-yd. run (Nugent kick)	4:55

—— OFFENSE ——

MICHIGAN

PASSING	ATT	COMP	YDS	INT	TD
Navarre	46	23	247	1	0
TEAM	2	0	0	0	0

RECEIVING	CATCHES	YDS	TD
Edwards	10	107	0
Bellamy	8	101	0
Askew	3	10	0
Joppru	2	29	0

RUSHING	RUSHES	YDS	TD
Perry	28	76	0
Askew	10	45	0
Navarre	3	0	0

OHIO STATE

PASSING	ATT	COMP	YDS	INT	TD
Krenzel	14	10	124	0	0

RECEIVING	CATCHES	YDS	TD
Jenkins	4	51	0
Clarett	2	35	0
Schnittker	1	15	0
Gamble	1	14	0
Vance	1	6	0
Ross	1	3	0

RUSHING	RUSHES	YDS	TD
Clarett	20	119	1
Krenzel	9	20	0
Hall	4	3	1
TEAM	1	-2	0

ABOVE:
Ohio State's Maurice Hall sprints toward the end zone for the game winning touchdown. (Dispatch photo by Mike Munden)

RIGHT:
Maurice Clarett celebrates teammate Maurice Hall's fourth-quarter touchdown. (Dispatch photo by Neal C. Lauron)

yard run to his first touchdown since the San Jose State game. It was his team-leading 16th TD of the year and gave the Buckeyes a 7-3 lead.

But the first half belonged to Michigan, ball-control-wise at least, as the Wolverines drove to three Adam Finley field goals. The third, a 22-yarder with 16 seconds left in the half, came at the end of a 19-play, 88-yard drive that ate 8:24.

The second half didn't belong to anyone until the Buckeyes took over in the fourth quarter at their 43 after Michigan's Brandon Williams was flagged for interfering with Chris Gamble on a punt catch. Krenzel went to work, with fullback Brandon Schnittker pulling down a pass obviously intended for Michael Jenkins and turning it into a 15-yard gain. Moments later, Hall, who scored the winning TD in overtime at Illinois the week before, did his thing.

Then it was the defense's turn. It turned away Michigan's first shot at answering when defensive end Darrion Scott forced quarterback John Navarre to give

up the first turnover of the game, a fumble Will Smith came up with at the OSU 36 with 2:02 left.

When OSU couldn't gain a first down, Andy Groom banged a 49-yard punt that Julius Curry returned to the Michigan 20. With 58 seconds left, the Wolverines had 80 yards to go, and a couple of passes to Ronald Bellamy and a pass interference call against Gamble helped them almost get there.

But with one second left and the ball at the OSU 24, Navarre fired a pass toward Braylon Edwards, slanting in from the left near the OSU goal line. Allen, one of three deep safeties on the play, moved in to grab the pass and end it.

"I knew No. 80 was going to be there, because he's their go-to guy," Allen said. "But they shouldn't have done it. They shouldn't have gone his way."

Bedlam reigned.

"It's a dream come true to get to this point," Wilhelm said. "We've obviously got one left, one big one left. We've attained some of the goals we talked about earlier in the season, but the big one is still left."

LEFT:
Ohio State's Brandon Schnittker is lifted up by fans after the victory over Michigan. The fullback caught a key pass in the game-winning drive.
(Dispatch photo by Mike Munden)

RIGHT:
Ohio State fans flood the field and climb the south goal post after the Buckeyes clinched a spot in the BCS national-championship game. (Dispatch photo by Barth Falkenberg)

LEFT:
Ohio State fans carry Buckeyes quarterback Craig Krenzel after Ohio State's win over Michigan.
(Dispatch photo by Karl Kuntz)

Ohio State fans flood on to the field and climb the south goal post after the Buckeyes clinched a spot at the BCS national championship in Tempe Arizona. (Dispatch photo by Barth Falkenberg)

Ohio Stadium erupts in celebration after the victory over Michigan.
(Dispatch photo by Karl Kuntz)

FRIDAY, JANUARY 3, 2003 — TEMPE, AZ

OHIO STATE VS MIAMI

A PERFECT ENDING

Buckeyes once again come up big when it counts to take title

BY TIM MAY

TEMPE, Ariz.—Cie Grant delivered the final uppercut for Ohio State last night in what will go down in history as one of college football's great upset knockouts.

The senior linebacker forced a bad pass by Miami quarterback Ken Dorsey on fourth down from the one-yard line in the second overtime. That made Maurice Clarett's five-yard touchdown run moments earlier the game winner in a 31-24 victory over the heavily favored Hurricanes. And it made the Buckeyes the national champions.

"It was two great heavyweights slugging it out, and our guys came up with the win," coach Jim Tressel said.

BELOW:
Buckeyes quarterback Craig Krenzel raises his arms in celebration after Ohio State topped Miami in overtime to win its first national championship since 1968. (Dispatch photo by Jeff Hinckley)

RIGHT:
Ohio State tailback Maurice Clarett celebrates in the end zone after scoring on a five-yard run in overtime that propelled the Buckeyes' to the national title. (Dispatch photo by Neal C. Lauron)

The rest of the Buckeyes and many of their fans charged the field and locked in a jubilant throng that enjoyed fireworks, confetti and hugs throughout. The rest of the predominantly OSU crowd of 77,502 in Sun Devil Stadium rocked in the glow of the school's first national championship since 1968 and the fifth overall. It capped the winningest season—14-0—in OSU history.

"We are so proud of these young men, these 13 seniors," Tressel said. "We've always had the best damn band in the land. Now we've got the best damn team in the land."

Miami had gone in as an 11-point favorite to become the first team to repeat as national champion since Nebraska in 1994 and '95. Instead, the Hurricanes, riding a 34-game winning streak, ran into the same OSU team that won any way it could—usually ugly—down the stretch of the season.

Miami coach Larry Coker watched the Buckeyes force five turnovers, converting two—a Mike Doss interception and a Kenny Peterson-forced fumble grabbed by Darrion Scott—into touchdowns as OSU took a 14-7 halftime lead.

BELOW:
Ohio State tailback Maurice Clarett dives into the end zone to score the eventual game-winning touchdown in overtime.
(Dispatch photo by Neal C. Lauron)

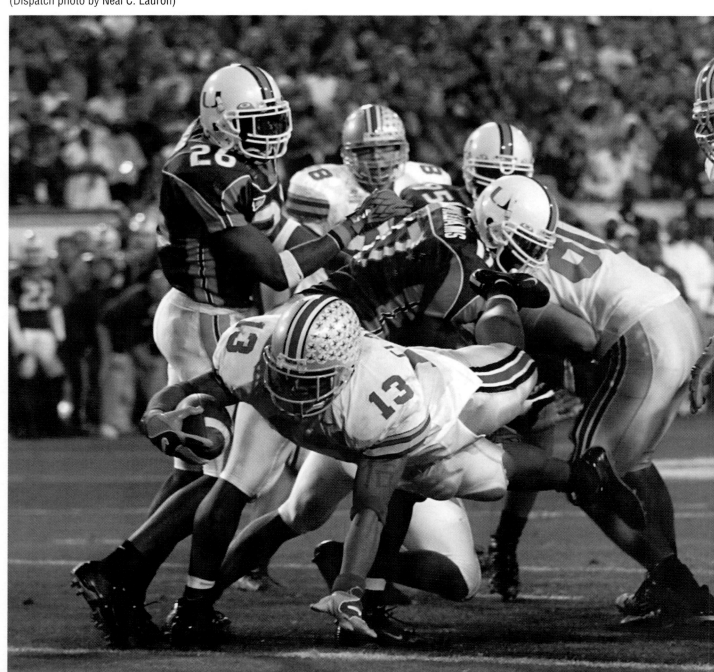

	1st	2nd	3rd	4th	OT1	OT2	Final
OHIO STATE	0	14	3	0	7	7	31
MIAMI	7	0	7	3	7	0	24

SCORING SUMMARY

QTR	TEAM	PLAY		TIME
1st	**Miami**	TD	Parrish 25-yd. pass from Dorsey (Sievers kick)	4:09
2nd	**Ohio State**	TD	Krenzel 1-yd. run (Nugent kick)	2:28
2nd	**Ohio State**	TD	Clarett 7-yd. run (Nugent kick)	1:10
3rd	**Ohio State**	FG	Nugent 44-yd. field goal	8:33
3rd	**Miami**	TD	McGahee 9-yd. run (Sievers kick)	2:11
4th	**Miami**	FG	Sievers 40-yd. field goal	0:00
OT1	**Miami**	TD	Winslow 7-yd. pass from Dorsey (Sievers kick)	0:00
OT1	**Ohio State**	TD	Krenzel 1-yd. run (Nugent kick)	0:00
OT2	**Ohio State**	TD	Clarett 5-yd. run (Nugent kick)	0:00

——— OFFENSE ———

OHIO STATE

PASSING	ATT	COMP	YDS	INT	TD
Krenzel	21	7	122	2	0

RECEIVING	CATCHES	YDS	TD
Jenkins	4	45	0
Gamble	2	69	0
Vance	1	8	0

RUSHING	RUSHES	YDS	TD
Krenzel	19	80	2
Clarett	22	47	2
Ross	10	17	0
Groom	1	0	0

MIAMI

PASSING	ATT	COMP	YDS	INT	TD
Dorsey	43	28	296	2	2
Crudup	1	1	7	0	0

RECEIVING	CATCHES	YDS	TD
Winslow	11	122	1
Parrish	5	70	1
Johnson	4	54	0
Sands	3	34	0
McGahee	3	5	0
Hill	1	7	0
Payton	1	7	0
Geathers	1	4	0

RUSHING	RUSHES	YDS	TD
McGahee	20	67	1
Payton	8	17	0
Hill	1	0	0
Dorsey	4	-16	0

ABOVE:
Buckeyes defender Cie Grant forces Miami quarterback Ken Dorsey into a hurried throw to end the game on the final play of the second overtime. (Dispatch photo by Chris Russell)

"They had that type of year all year," said Coker, who suffered his first defeat in his two years as Miami's coach. "They are a great football team, well coached and extremely hard to fight."

The game had moved to overtime after Miami kicker Todd Sievers nailed a 40-yard field goal on the final play of regulation to tie the score at 17. It came just as the Buckeyes appeared ready to put the game away. But Miami's Roscoe Parrish took a punt back 50 yards to the OSU 26 to set up the kick.

Miami struck first in OT, with Dorsey flipping a lob to tight end Kellen Winslow Jr. over the head of safety Will Allen.

The Buckeyes came back for the tying score behind quarterback Craig Krenzel, the offensive player of the game. They survived two fourth downs to do it. Facing fourth and 14 from the 29, Krenzel hit Michael Jenkins with a pass to the 12. Then, on fourth and three from the five, Miami's Glenn Sharpe was called for pass interference while covering Chris Gamble in the end zone

That put the ball at the two. Krenzel sneaked in from a yard out on third down, and after an illegal-procedure call, kicker Mike Nugent delivered the tying point.

The Buckeyes drove to Clarett's five-yard scoring run to start the second OT, then put up a goal-line stand led by linebacker Matt Wilhelm that forced the final play from the one-yard line. Grant raced in, and the 2002 Ohio State team zoomed into history.

"Everyone should cherish this, because you're never guaranteed to come back here," Grant said. "The last team to do this at Ohio State was 1968. Look at all the great players who have come and gone in between."

He'll have his name wedged in there someplace, as will many members of the OSU defense. Some critics said the vaunted unit would be overmatched by the speed and diversity of Miami, featuring Dorsey, running back Willis McGahee, wide receiver Andre Johnson and Winslow.

Allen's hit on McGahee with 11:39 left in the fourth quarter sent the star to the sideline with a knee injury, and Wilhelm's hit on Dorsey in overtime sent the quarterback to the sideline for a play. Johnson had four catches for 54 yards.

Winslow turned out to be the toughest, catching a Miami bowl-record 11 passes for 122 yards. Whether Dorsey—he was 28 of 43 for 296 yards, two interceptions and two TDs—was looking for Winslow on the final play wasn't known. Grant's pressure made it a moot point.

Krenzel gained his offensive player of the game award not for style but for tenacity. He was seven of 21 passing for 122 yards with two interceptions. But he ran for a career-high 81 yards on 19 carries and scored twice on sneaks.

BELOW:
Ohio State's Dustin Fox celebrates after an interception against Miami in the second quarter. (Dispatch photo by Neal C. Lauron)

It also wasn't the greatest rushing day in Clarett's young career—he was held to 47 yards on 23 carries. But he still scored two TDs and delivered the most bizarre play of the game.

Midway through the third quarter, Miami's Sean Taylor picked off a Krenzel pass in the end zone and headed toward the left sideline before being caught by Clarett, who pulled the ball from Taylor's arms at the OSU 28.

Four plays later, Nugent made a 44-yard field goal to give OSU a 17-7 lead.

That lead didn't last. The Hurricanes finished off a seven-play, 60-yard drive with a nine-yard TD run by McGahee and then used the field goal by Sievers to send it to OT.

While that was a place where Ohio State had been just two games earlier in the win at Illinois, Miami had never been there throughout its 34-game winning streak.

"It's no different than what we've done all year," Krenzel said. "We made plays when we had to."

LEFT:
Ohio State quarterback Craig Krenzel falls into the end zone to score a touchdown in overtime.
(Dispatch photo by Chris Russell)

ABOVE:
Ohio State's Brandon Mitchell celebrates against Miami in the second quarter of the Fiesta Bowl.
(Dispatch photo by Chris Russell)

IT'S NO DIFFERENT THAN WHAT WE'VE DONE ALL YEAR, WE MADE PLAYS WHEN WE HAD TO.

—OHIO STATE QUARTERBACK
CRAIG KRENZEL

LEFT:
Buckeyes coach Jim Tressel, quarterback Craig Krenzel and the Buckeyes celebrate their national championship. (Dispatch photo by Jeff Hinckley)

LEFT:
Ohio State's Alex Stepanovich (left) and Kenny Peterson celebrate with the Fiesta Bowl trophy.
(Dispatch photo by Jeff Hinckley)

BELOW:
Ohio State coach Jim Tressel hands the Circuit City national championship trophy to defensive tackle Kenny Peterson (Dispatch photo by Jeff Hinckley)

RIGHT:
Maurice Clarett celebrates after he pulled the ball from the hands of Sean Taylor.
(Dispatch photo by Fred Squillante)

BUCKEYES REGULAR-SEASON STATISTICS

OFFENSE

PASSING

PLAYER	ATT	CMP	PCT	YDS	TD	INT
Craig Krenzel	228	141	61.8	1988	12	5
Scott McMullen	31	25	80.6	315	2	0

RECEIVING

PLAYER	ATT	YDS	TD
Michael Jenkins	57	1031	6
Chris Gamble	29	430	0
Chris Vance	12	170	3
Drew Carter	10	147	0
Ben Hartsock	17	137	2
Maurice Clarett	12	104	2
Lydell Ross	10	75	0
Redgie Arden	4	50	0
Brandon Childress	4	7	0
Maurice Hall	5	43	0
Ryan Hamby	2	29	1
Brandon Schnittker	2	27	0
John Hollins	1	14	0
Scott McMullen	1	-1	0

RUSHING

PLAYER	ATT	YDS	TD
Maurice Clarett	199	1190	14
Lydell Ross	157	602	6
Maurice Hall	78	370	4
Craig Krenzel	106	287	1
Chris Gamble	3	49	1
JaJa Riley	12	44	0
Donnie Nickey	1	28	0
Roshawn Parker	1	6	0
Jim Otis	1	2	0
Scott McMullen	4	1	1
Branden Joe	1	1	0
Brandon Schnittker	1	1	0
Andy Groom	1	-16	0

SPECIAL TEAMS

FIELD GOALS

PLAYER	1-19	20-29	30-39	40-49	50+
Mike Nugent	0/0	6/6	9/10	8/9	1/1

PUNTING

PLAYER	NO	AVG	INSIDE 20
Andy Groom	54	44.6	14

PUNT RETURNS

PLAYER	NO	YDS	AVG	TD
Chris Gamble	34	292	8.6	0
Mike Doss	4	25	6.2	0
Donnie Nickey	1	14	14.0	0
Michael Jenkins	1	11	11.0	0
Dustin Fox	1	10	10.0	0
Chris Vance	1	5	5.0	0

KICKOFF RETURNS

PLAYER	NO	YDS	AVG	TD
Maurice Hall	18	419	23.3	0
Chris Gamble	11	253	23.0	0
Mike Doss	2	37	18.5	0
Brandon Joe	2	10	5.0	0
Chris Vance	1	2	2.0	0
Jack Tucker	1	0	0.0	0
Brandon Schnittker	1	11	11.0	0

DEFENSE

TACKLES

PLAYER	NO	SOLO	AST
Matt Wilhelm	111	73	38
Mike Doss	98	62	36
Dustin Fox	77	62	15
Cie Grant	64	46	18
Donnie Nickey	62	41	21
Robert Reynolds	58	36	22
Will Smith	51	35	16
Darrion Scott	42	21	21

PLAYER	NO	SOLO	AST
David Thompson	39	23	16
Kenny Peterson	38	22	16
Tim Anderson	32	15	17
Will Allen	27	19	8
A.J. Hawk	26	13	13
E.J. Underwood	21	17	4
Chris Gamble	19	18	1
Simon Fraser	19	12	7
Richard McNutt	16	10	6
Bobby Carpenter	12	8	4
Mike Kudla	11	5	6
Fred Pagac	11	8	3
Tyler Everett	10	6	4
Chris Conwell	8	7	1
Bobby Britton	7	3	4
Mike D'Andrea	7	4	3
Harlen Jacobs	6	6	0
Nate Salley	6	3	3
Jason Bond	4	2	2
Bam Childress	3	2	1
Pat O'Neill	2	2	0
Jack Tucker	2	1	1
Steven Moore	2	2	0
Marcus Green	2	1	1
Team	2	1	1
Craig Krenzel	1	1	0
Andy Groom	1	1	0
Kyle Andrews	1	1	0
Redgie Arden	1	0	1
Mike Nugent	1	1	0
Nate Stead	1	1	0
Nick Mangold	1	1	0
Brandon Schnittker	1	1	0
David Andrews	1	1	0

SACKS

PLAYER	NO	PLAYER	NO
Darrion Scott	8.5	Matt Wilhelm	3.0
Will Smith	4.5	Tim Anderson	2.5
David Thompson	4.5	Robert Reynolds	1.0
Cie Grant	4.0	Will Allen	1.0
Kenny Peterson	4.0	A.J. Hawk	0.5
Simon Fraser	4.0		

INTERCEPTIONS

PLAYER	NO	YDS	AVG	TD
Chris Gamble	4	40	10.0	1
A.J. Hawk	2	44	22.0	1
Matt Wilhelm	2	0	0.0	0
Will Allen	2	0	0.0	0
Dustin Fox	2	0	0.0	0
Mike Doss	1	45	45.0	1
Cie Grant	1	23	23.0	0
Will Smith	1	0	0.0	0
Tyler Everett	1	0	0.0	0

TEAM

	BUCKEYES	OPP
Scoring	379	159
Points per game	29.2	12.2
Touchdowns	44	16
First downs	231	224
Rushing	126	69
Passing	100	141
Penalty	5	14
Net yards rushing	2533	1023
Net yards passing	2303	3100
FGM/FGA	24/26	16/23

The entire staff of the *Columbus Dispatch* sports and photo departments contributed to the coverage of the Buckeyes' 2002 season. We gratefully acknowledge the efforts of:

SPORTS DEPARTMENT:
TIM MAY
BOB HUNTER
AARON PORTZLINE
TODD JONES
RAY STEIN
SCOTT PRIESTLE
BOB BAPTIST
ROB OLLER
SCOTT DAVIS

PHOTOGRAPHY DEPARTMENT:
NEAL LAURON
JEFF HINCKLEY
ALYSIA PEYTON
MIKE MUNDEN
BARTH FALKENBERG
FRED SQUILLANTE
ROBERT CAPLIN
ERIC ALBRECHT
CHRIS RUSSELL
TIM REVELL
DORAL CHENOWETH, III